THE CHARACTER OF THE BLESSED

The Power of the Reborn Spirit

J9:
I Call you Blessed:

1 cor 13:8

[signature]

The Character of the Blessed
ISBN 978-1-939570-12-3

Copyright © 2013
by Dr. Billy J. Rash

Billy Rash Ministries
7850 White Lane, No. 117
Bakersfield, California 93309

Published by Word & Spirit Publishing
P.O. Box 701403
Tulsa, OK 74170

THE CHARACTER OF THE BLESSED

The Power of the Reborn Spirit

BY DR. BILLY J. RASH

DEDICATION

This book is dedicated to my faithful congregation at Kern Christian Center in Bakersfield, California who exemplify the hearts of true disciples. Thank you for your love and support.

CONTENTS

FOREWORD

The human man or human being is an integrated system made up of spirit, soul and physical body or flesh. You don't have a spirit; you are a spirit. You have a soul made up of your mind, your will and your emotions. You live and have life in a physical body. The body is totally dependent on the spirit for its life force in this earth. Jesus said it like this in John 6:63, *"It is the spirit that quickeneth; the flesh profiteth nothing: the words that I speak unto you, they are spirit, and they are life."*

Our quality of life while we're in the earth depends on how well these three main systems work together. The spirit, or the real man, must be born again by the Holy Spirit. The mind, then, must be renewed by the Word of God in order for the will and the emotions to become stable and free from fear. That, then, brings healing and peace to the body. None of this can be done without The Living Word of God.

I've been in this ministry for 46+ years, and it still amazes me how many good people make bad decisions because of a lack of time spent in The Word. Jesus said in John 8:31 the only way one can be His disciple is to continue in His Word. Then the disciple, you or me or anyone else, will know the truth and THE TRUTH will make you free. Far too many Christians are going from Sunday to Sunday without the Word of God having any effect on their lives or decisions. This must change. NOW! The book you are about to read will help you get the system working in harmony as it should be—a strong spirit full of faith working with a sound fear-free mind through a healed, well body.

I know Billy Rash well. I've watched him grow through the things that it takes to be a true disciple of Jesus. Follow him as he follows Jesus through every page of *The Character of the Blessed*. Your life on the victory side is there for you. Take it! Don't ever let go of it.

Jesus is Lord!

Kenneth Copeland

THE CHARACTER OF THE BLESSED

INTRODUCTION

In Matthew, chapters 5, 6, and 7, Jesus delivers a profound teaching called the Sermon on the Mount. For purposes of our study, we will focus on the first portion of the Sermon on the Mount found in Matthew chapter 5, verses 3 through 12.

When reading these verses, you may think Jesus is randomly listing characteristics every Christian should have. Not so. They are characteristics, yes, but they are ones you cannot possibly possess on your own, and they can only be possessed by true disciples. They are a progression of godly characteristics that can only be reached and maintained through a constant relationship with the Father. As you mature, one characteristic develops into the next. It is a spiritual progression.

These characteristics, described by our Lord Jesus, are not only systematic and purposeful in their order, but they are answers to questions posed by the prophets of old. Jesus truly had the wisdom of God while on earth. It is only through godly wisdom and the help of the Holy Spirit that such detailed and intricate instructions could be given so concisely.

Early publishers of the Bible dubbed these Scriptures the "Beatitudes." However, this is a man-made term and lends itself to the belief that these are simply "attitudes" every

Christian should "be." While they may be good attitudes to have, such an interpretation minimizes what Jesus is actually saying, and the instructions He is giving.

First, these characteristics can only be developed in true disciples, not all Christians. And when you develop these characteristics in the presence of the Father, you will be BLESSED. Further, these characteristics may be more than they appear to be on the surface. In this study, we will look at many of these terms in the Greek in order to better comprehend the goodness of God that is so beautifully illustrated in Matthew 5:3-12. In verses 3 through 9, Jesus gives us the character of disciples walking in the blessing; in verses 10 through 12, that character is put to the test by the reaction of the world.

As you delve into these characteristics of the blessed, I assure you, it will be like finding the chocolate center of a Tootsie Pop; it is that sweet spot you will not want to leave— the secret place of the Most High (Ps. 91:1). For it is by having the "character of the blessed" that you obtain the wisdom to take on everything life (and every demon from hell) tries to throw at you. Be prepared! Become a true disciple by walking in the *Character of the Blessed.*

CHAPTER 1

THE ISSUES OF LIFE

A term that is used by so many people in this day and hour is "issues." On the television, everyone is talking about *issues*. As a pastor, what I hear from people more than anything else is *"I have issues."* They would have come to church, they say, but *"I had issues."* They assure me that they would have done this or that, but again, they had issues.

In this chapter, we will address the **issues of life**. But, our focus will be on biblical issues—not worldly issues. The world's issues are generally bad news for which they have no answers. One of the greatest things about the Word of God is that it does not leave us uninformed in any area. Any issues you and I face can be answered in the Word. We are going to find out how to allow godly issues to set the course in our lives and determine our future instead of worldly issues.

Look at Proverbs 4:23:

> *Keep your heart with all diligence, for out of it spring **the issues of life**.*

The *Amplified Bible* reads this way:

> *Keep and guard your heart with all vigilance and above all that you guard, for out of it flow **the springs of life**.*

God is urging us to guard our hearts. Although it is essential to take care of one's physical body and health, God is not talking about your body's blood pump. He is talking about the heart of your being—the place where your core belief system is stored. As a believer, your heart is your recreated, born-again spirit, and the place from which faith springs forth with power.

What you have faith in will become your reality— good or bad.

The guarding of your heart is essential because the "issues" and "springs" of life" flowing from your recreated spirit are spiritual forces that affect and form your character. They are spiritual forces with an unseen power that build a wall of blessings around you, much like the hedge of protection that was placed around Job by God (Job 1:10). The more your faith develops the stronger your wall becomes. Yet, these forces are not blessings that come from heaven, but they actually spring forth from your own reborn spirit. The more the blessing flows out the more faith is developed. That is why God says to guard it with all diligence, because what you have faith in will become your reality—good or bad.

The *New Living Translation* makes a very good point, and it says this:

> *Guard your heart above all else, for it determines the course of your life.*

Has it occurred to you that the issues of life that you face are the result of your own thought life? The Scripture says to *"guard your heart"* because it determines *"the course of your life."* In order to guard our hearts, we must guard our **thought life**.

For as he [a man or woman] *thinks in his heart, so is he. "Eat and drink!" he says to you, but his heart is not with you.*

Proverbs 23:7

Some theologians say this verse refers to the purchase of food and drink and uses the word "heart" in general terms. However, when you search this Scripture out in the Greek and Hebrew, you discover a more accurate interpretation would be "as a man thinks in his heart, so is he."

Consider the *Today's English Version*:

"Come on and have some more," he says, but he doesn't mean it. ***What he thinks is what he really is.***

Without much effort, what you think and how your thought process works, gets down into your heart. As this happens, what you are thinking manifests into *who you become* because you believe it to be true. You see, now your faith kicks in. You believe it. Subsequently, this affects *who you are* because what you think in your heart you become (Prov. 23:7), and out of your heart springs forth the course and issues of your life (Prov. 4:23).

Guard Your Heart

What you think in your heart, or reborn spirit, is what you are. And since we have discovered that out of your heart flow the issues of life, GUARD YOUR HEART! How do you guard your heart? By filling it with God's Word, and not with what the news media says, what your boss says, or what your neighbor says. FILL YOUR HEART WITH GOD'S WORD. Meditate and ponder on that Word because when the storms of life hit, it is God's issues or course you want to flow out as a hedge of protection, and not some worldly junk you saw on the news.

You may ask, "Are you telling me what's going wrong in my life is coming out of my own heart?" That is exactly what I am telling you. Further, how you *respond* to what is going on in your life also flows out of your heart. Because, as we have learned, out of your heart flows the issues of life, and what flows out of your heart determines the course of your life. How you respond or deal with the issues springing forth in your life is called CHARACTER.

Godly Character

Your character, when dealing with the issues of life, is revealed by your response to those issues. Your character is not revealed when everything is going great. Your true character is shown, and what is truly in your heart is revealed, when someone or something puts pressure on you.

For example, if someone resorts to substance abuse, stealing, or lying when difficulties hit, you might say they have a weak character. It is when someone walks uprightly when the pressure is on that a strong or godly character is revealed.

Further, there is a process through which your character manifests: As you think about, meditate, ponder, and turn over and over in your mind the issues of your life, those thoughts penetrate your heart. When this occurs, if you do not *guard your heart* to ensure that your thoughts are in agreement with the Word of God, you will start thinking and acting like the man in Proverbs 23:7. That is he says what seems to be the *right* thing to say, but deep in his heart he thinks something else. And what he thinks, the Scripture says, is what he really is.

When you find yourself pondering thoughts that are contrary to the Word of God, reject them immediately. Otherwise, you will become double minded. James declares that a double-minded man is unstable in all his ways (James 1:8).

In fact, when you act in a way that is contradictory to your actual beliefs, then your character has weakened. What is flowing out of your heart is not based on God's Word. More than likely, your thoughts have become dominated with the issues of life, which will bring out of your heart courses that are contrary to the Word. Subsequently, this leaves you with a flimsy character that responds to pressurized circumstances without a hint of God's Word.

Guard Your Thoughts

How do you stop this progression? It all begins in the thought phase.

(1) What you ponder and think about gets into your heart.

(2) What is in your heart flows out of you.

(3) What flows out of you determines your character.

When you find yourself pondering thoughts that are contrary to the Word of God, and I understand those thoughts can be strong, say, "I rebuke that thought in the name of Jesus. I only say what my heavenly Father says about this situation." Then proceed to quote what the Bible says about your situation. If you do not know what the Word says, then get yourself a good topical Scripture key book and find out what God says about it.

Jesus Teaches About Character

With this all in mind, let us see what Jesus teaches about character and the issues facing us in our daily lives. You may not know this, but **Jesus has dealt with every issue you will ever face**. There is nothing new under the sun. There is no *new* pressure.

If you think you are the only one in the world who is going through something, I am here to tell you, Jesus has already taught, dealt with, and given us instructions on how to think and how to deal with the issues of life. How so? **It is all about your character.** It is how you respond to the issues of life that is key, and not a double-minded response like the man we saw in Proverbs 23. You want your *heart* to

Jesus has dealt with every issue you will ever face.

line up with your *words*, and you want *those words* to line up with *God's Word*.

It is operating in that kind of godly character that allows the blessing to flow from your heart. And it all begins with the thoughts you allow to go into your heart—that subsequently flow out, and determine your character and the issues of life surrounding you.

As we will discover in the Chapters to come, Jesus teaches us how to deal with the issues of life and develop a godly character. THERE ARE NO EXCEPTIONS TO HIS METHODS. THERE ARE NO SHORTCUTS. It does not matter where on this earth you live—the same principles, the same character, and the same thought life apply. If thoughts contrary to God's Word get into your heart, then they will have a negative effect on you.

What you will discover is that the *Character of the Blessed* is not something God will send you from heaven as your character develops. No, you already have the *Character of the Blessed* on the inside of your born-again spirit—it just has to be developed and brought forth! Praise God! As a believer, all the answers to your issues of life are already on the inside of you.

CHAPTER 2

HOW TO DEAL WITH THE ISSUES OF LIFE

I n Matthew, chapters 5, 6, and 7, Jesus instructs His disciples concerning numerous issues and circumstances they will face. This collection of Scriptures is called the **Sermon on the Mount**. However, it is not really a sermon, but Jesus teaching His disciples about character and how to deal with the issues of everyday life. Within those Scriptures, Jesus covers all of today's issues.

A subpart of the Sermon on the Mount, specifically Matthew chapter 5, verses 3-12, is a popular set of verses often referred to as the **Beatitudes**. The word *beatitude* is a term that men created. Personally, I have never been quite sure what a beatitude is except for, perhaps, an attitude you should be in. However, what Jesus sets forth are not attitudes.

Jesus begins verses 3 through 11 with the word *BLESSED*, and He is talking about the blessing of God flowing out of your heart as an issue of life as we discussed in Chapter 1. It is a blessing! It is empowerment to live, in this earth, with the blessing flowing out of your heart as God intended.

The Sermon on the Mount

Jesus teaches His disciples about the issues of life they will face.

While we will discuss Matthew 5:3-12 in more detail later, let us first look at the Sermon on the Mount, collectively Matthew chapters 5, 6, and 7. In fact, go ahead and get your Bible out and read those three chapters. As you do, notice Jesus' continuous flow from one chapter to the next. And remember, it is not really a sermon, but a gathering on a mountain where Jesus teaches His disciples about the issues of life they will face.

Jesus Identifies True Disciples

Throughout these chapters, Jesus never changes the subject or who He is addressing. He does not take a break, and He does not leave that location and go to another. It is one continuous flow of teaching to His target audience: **His disciples**. Then, as the teaching closes in chapter 7, Jesus separates the true and false disciples.

Let us examine Matthew 7:21-23 more closely in the *New Living Translation*:

True Disciples

*"Not everyone who calls out to me, 'Lord! Lord!' will enter the Kingdom of Heaven. **Only those who actually do the will of my Father in heaven will enter.** On judgment day many will say to me, 'Lord! Lord! We prophesied in your name and cast out demons in your name and performed many miracles in your name.'*

*"But I will reply, 'I never knew you. Get away from me, **you who break God's laws.'"***

Notice, there are two types of disciples: (1) those who do the will of the Father, and (2) those who break God's laws. In other words, if a disciple is not doing the will of the Father, he or she is breaking God's laws.

Now, notice the description used above the passage is "True Disciples." The *New International Version* says, "True and False Disciples," while *The New Jerusalem Bible* says, "The True Disciple." So, Matthew 7:21-23 is speaking to Jesus' disciples, and then separates the true and false disciples.

Not Every Christian is a Disciple

The entire, continuous flow of the Sermon on the Mount is Jesus teaching His disciples (Matt. 5:1-7:27), and Jesus pinpoints the identity of true disciples as those who actually do the will of His Father in heaven (Matt. 7:21). Jesus is not talking to everyone. He is only talking to His disciples.

In fact, I will go ahead and tell you, in these three chapters of Matthew, Jesus is ONLY talking to His disciples, and NOT every Christian. "What are you saying Pastor Billy? Are you saying that the Sermon on the Mount and the Beatitudes that I was taught in Sunday school aren't for all Christians?" Well, read on and find out for yourself.

In order to investigate this premise properly, we need to go back to the beginning of Jesus' teaching on the mountain to His disciples. Matthew 5:1-2 reads as follows:

> *And seeing the multitudes, He went up on a mountain, and when He was seated His **disciples** came to Him.*

Notice the whole multitude did not come to Him. Not even those closest to the mountain came to Him. The Scripture says *"His disciples came to Him."* Further, we really do not know how many disciples there were. **By disciples, it does not mean just the twelve apostles.** It was most likely a large crowd of disciples. But, the Scripture says they were disciples.

Verse 2 goes on to say He began teaching the disciples:

Then He opened His mouth and taught them [the disciples], *saying:*

So, we have recognized that Jesus is not talking to the multitudes of people following Him. In Matthew 5:3, Jesus begins teaching His disciples about character, the issues of life, and the blessing. He never stops talking to His disciples. Therefore, the Sermon on the Mount (Matt. 5, 6, and 7), which includes the Beatitudes (Matt. 5:3-12), does not apply to everyone who calls themself a Christian, and it is not going to be followed by those who just THINK they are a Christian.

Jesus' teachings in Matthew chapters 5, 6, and 7 will only be followed and obeyed by those who are dedicated disciples. Of course, He is not singling out the disciples. Every Christian can choose to become a disciple, and I hope that you do. What Jesus is saying is "This is how a true disciple is going to be in life," and then He begins teaching on the issues of life. It is true disciples who walk in the blessing.

What is a True Disciple?

In order to fully grasp what Jesus is teaching, we must understand what a disciple is. To do that, we must go to the original Greek translation.

1. True Disciples are Learners.

In the Greek, the word *disciple* is *mathetes*. According to *Vine's Expository Dictionary*, the first definition of a *disciple* is "a learner." That seems simple. In order to be a true disciple, you have to want to learn, and continue to learn. We never fully arrive as disciples of Jesus when it comes to studying and learning. A *learner* means "always learning from the Word."

Of course, you always have your "know it all's." **Find me someone who thinks they have arrived and you will find someone who has slipped away from being a true disciple.**

I have been in the ministry for over 30 years, but that does not mean I have stopped learning or putting myself in positions to learn. My wife, Shelby, and I still go to Believers' Conventions to study and learn. We have to get the Word.

After we return home from an out-of-town meeting, I always have people come up to us and say, "Did you enjoy your vacation?"

"Vacation?" I reply. "Are you kidding me?"

Most meetings have five or six sessions a day, and for all six days. AND THE NOTES! My goodness, the notes I take.

What is being taught about the Word is always so good that I find myself writing pages and pages of notes. And you have to write fast. You know how quickly some of these on-fire preachers can talk!

So, a true disciple is someone who is a learner, and one who continues to learn from the Word. It does not matter how many times you have heard the Word, you must keep learning. We do not get faith by *having heard* the Word. Faith comes by *hearing* the Word *constantly* (Rom. 10:17).

> *A true disciple is one who continues to learn from the Word.*

2. True Disciples Follow Jesus.

Vine's second definition of a *disciple* is "one who follows the teachings of another."

Unfortunately, not everyone who says they are a Christian actually follows the teachings of Jesus. In order to be a true disciple, you have to learn and follow your teacher. That is why on judgment day there will be disciples who say they did this and that, but Jesus will say He never knew them. Let us look at that Scripture again.

True Disciples

> *"Not everyone who calls out to me, 'Lord! Lord!' will enter the Kingdom of Heaven. Only those who actually do the will of my Father in heaven will enter. On judgment day many will say to me, 'Lord! Lord! We*

prophesied in your name and cast out demons in your name and performed many miracles in your name.'

"But I will reply, 'I never knew you. Get away from me, you who break God's laws.'"

Matthew 7:21-23, NLT

Even though some of the disciples perform many miracles in Jesus' name, they are not true disciples because they break God's laws. However, those who follow Jesus' teachings and live in accordance with them are His true disciples.

*So Jesus said to those Jews who had believed in Him, If you abide in My word **[hold fast to My teachings and live in accordance with them], you are truly My disciples.***

John 8:31, AMP

In order to follow after the ways of Jesus and be a true disciple, there are things you must develop in your life, in your thought process, and in your character. Who you really are in your heart must coincide with your words and deeds. To do this, you must **abide in the Word**.

Remember, we learned in Chapter 1 that your thought process determines who you are. What you think goes into your heart, and out of your heart flow the issues of life. This process determines your character and issues in your own life. In order to control your thought process and the data you put into your heart effectively, you must abide in His Word and His Word abide in you. As the Word abides in you, it affects every aspect of your character, and then you can go and put it to work.

3. True Disciples are Doers of the Word.

Vine's third definition of a *disciple* is one who is "not only a pupil, but an adherent," or one who actually adheres to the teaching. That means actually **doing** what the Word says.

Simply learning the Word of God is not enough. A Muslim, Hindu, or even an atheist can *learn* the Word if they set their minds to it.

A true disciple is a person who *learns* and *follows* the Word of God. They are not hearers only, but doers of the Word and adherents to the Word. Interestingly, *Vine's* terms Jesus' followers in this definition as "His adherents."

4. True Disciples are Imitators of Jesus.

A fourth definition of a *disciple* is "one who imitates the teacher." In order to imitate Jesus, we must:

(1) Learn the Word,

(2) Abide in the Word, and

(3) Do the Word.

5. True Disciples Train to be Mature.

A final definition of a *disciple* is "one who is under authority for training for the purpose of being brought to maturity." True disciples desire to be brought to maturity in word and deed.

Definition of a True Disciple

If we put everything together that we now know about disciples, here is our working definition: **A true disciple is one who constantly learns from the Word, abides in that Word, does the Word, desires to be Christ-like, and wants to mature in word and deed.**

That is a true disciple! And according to Matthew 5:1-2, these are the people Jesus is addressing when He begins His teaching called the Sermon on the Mount. At the end of the teaching, Jesus gives crucial instructions on how to maintain a true discipleship: By actually doing what He is teaching, which is the will of His heavenly Father. If they do not—if they are just running around playing church and not doing the Father's will—Jesus says they are breaking God's laws. On judgment day, He will say to them, "I never knew you. Get away from Me."

If you are thinking, "Well, I'm only three out of five of those definitions," or "I'm only one out of those five," or maybe "I'm none of those." I have good news for you. You CAN BE ALL FIVE because Jesus did not lay it all out for us to remain ignorant, and He did not make it unobtainable. Every one of us CAN and SHOULD BE disciples.

Jesus Defines True Disciples

We have identified a true disciple by going to the Greek and defining the word *disciple*. Now let us examine Jesus' criteria for a true disciple.

1. True Disciples Abide in the Word.

> *Then Jesus said to those Jews who believed Him. "If you abide in My word, you are My disciples indeed."*
>
> John 8:31

It is impossible to be a true disciple without abiding in the Word. This does not mean you are not a Christian if you do not abide in the Word, nor does it mean you do not *desire* to be a true disciple; however, if you are going to be a true disciple, you must abide in the Word.

2. True Disciples Leave All.

> *Now great multitudes went with Him. And He turned and said to them, "If anyone comes to Me and does not hate his father and mother, wife and children, brothers and sisters, yes, and his own life also, he cannot be My disciple."*
>
> Luke 14:25-26

What is Jesus saying here? By using the word *hate,* he is not talking literally about hating and despising your family.

What He is saying is that if you are going to be His true disciple, you must be willing to leave all.

Jesus did not say you **have to** leave all, but you must be **willing to** leave all in order to be a true disciple. It is a willingness of the heart.

3. True Disciples Bear Their Cross.

> *"And whoever does not bear his cross and come after Me cannot be My disciple."*
>
> Luke 14:27

By saying "his cross," Jesus does not mean you must bear HIS cross, as in Jesus' cross. No, Jesus says a disciple must bear HIS OWN cross.

Let me give you some good news. No one in the world can bear the cross that our Lord Jesus Christ bore. If we could have, there would have been no need for Him to come on our behalf. What this Scripture is saying is you will have to die to yourself, to a degree, if you are going to be a disciple.

In order to get a better understanding of this Scripture, look at Matthew 11:28-29. Jesus says,

> *"Come to Me, all you who labor and are heavy laden, and I will give you rest. Take My yoke upon you and learn from Me, for I am gentle and lowly in heart, and you will find rest for your souls."*

Jesus is saying that if you do not take up your cross, deny yourself, and follow Him, then you will not have a part in Him.

Your "cross" is you denying yourself so you can learn of Him.

Your "cross" is you denying yourself so you can learn of Him. If you are going to be a true disciple, it is going to take your time. It already takes some of your time when you come to church. But, I pray that going to church is not the only time you have with the Lord. If so, although we pastors are doing the best we can, you are underfed! You need more than just an hour on Wednesday and two hours on Sunday, or whenever your church holds services. You need more!

The cross of a true disciple is to deny oneself and learn of Him.

I understand that teaching to deny oneself, dying to self, and taking up your cross is not a popular message anymore. We live in a self-infatuated and self-gratifying society wherein everything is about making us feel good. That is why there are seeker-friendly churches that would not DARE mention a cost or even the cross because it might make you uncomfortable.

But to my congregation, and to those reading this book, I fully intend for you to be uncomfortable if you are not a true disciple. My assignment from God, as a member of the five-fold ministry, is for the perfecting of the saints for the work of the ministry.

> *And He Himself gave some to be apostles, some prophets, some evangelists, and some pastors and teachers, for the equipping of the saints for the work of ministry . . . till we all come to the unity of the faith and of the knowledge of the Son of God, to a perfect man . . . that we should no longer be children, tossed to and fro and carried about with every wind of doctrine . . . but, speaking the truth in love, may grow up in all things into Him, who is the head—Christ.*

Ephesians 4:11-15

My job is to equip you for the work of the ministry so you can become mature, and then help others to become mature. In order for such maturity to manifest, it is going to take everything outlined in this book, and it is going to cost you. It is going to cost everyone who commits to become a true disciple and bear their own cross by denying themselves and learning of Him.

4. True Disciples Count the Cost.

What have we seen so far? Jesus says it is impossible to be a true disciple without (1) abiding in the Word, (2) be willing to leave everything (family and all), (3) bearing or carrying your own cross (denying yourself and learning of Him), and now (4) counting the cost. Jesus says,

"For which of you, intending to build a tower, does not sit down first and count the cost, whether he has enough to finish it.

". . . Or what king, going to make war against another king, does not sit down first and consider whether he is able with ten thousand to meet him who comes against him with twenty thousand?"

Luke 14:28, 31

In other words, count the cost beforehand. Do not put your hand to the plow and get halfway down the furrow and decide, "You know, I don't like this." Count the cost ahead of time.

If you are thinking you are fine and that you meet all the criteria of a true disciple, consider the following. Jesus says,

"So likewise, whoever of you does not forsake all that he has cannot be My disciple."

Luke 14:33

Let me stop here for a moment and make sure you realize that neither I nor Jesus is teaching **asceticism**. Asceticism is a theology that teaches the poorer and more without material possessions you are, the more holy and Christ-like you are. Such theology is why you have monks living in monasteries and denying everything going on in the world. Although they may have a great relationship with the Lord, they are very selfish because no one is receiving help from them.

Asceticism is a belief that a disciple should have nothing. Such is a deceptive belief, and it comes from a poverty spirit. It is saying, "The less I have then the more like Jesus I am," and that is NOT what Jesus is teaching.

The Rich Young Ruler

Recall, the rich young ruler that comes to Jesus and asks what he can do to inherit eternal life. Jesus says to him,

> *"You know the commandments: 'Do not commit adultery,' 'Do not murder,' 'Do not steal,' 'Do not bear false witness,' 'Do not defraud,' 'Honor your father and your mother.'"*
>
> *And he answered and said to Him, "Teacher, all these things I have kept from my youth."*
>
> *Then Jesus, looking at him, loved him, and said to him. "One thing you lack: Go your way, sell whatever you have and give to the poor . . ."*

Mark 10:19-21

Now, that is generally where everyone stops reading and says, "See there. If he had given everything away, then he could have been a disciple." That may be partially true, but that is not what Jesus is really saying. Continuing on in verse 21, Jesus says,

> *". . . sell whatever you have and give to the poor,* ***and you will have treasure in heaven;*** *and come, take up the cross, and follow Me."*

Why are those words left out? It sounds like an exchange to me. Jesus tells him to sell everything he owns, give to the poor, AND he will have treasure in heaven. Yes, we must be *willing* to sell or forsake all, but if we obey Him, then we shall HAVE.

Jesus says when you forsake all for Him, you will have treasure laid up in heaven. That does not mean you are laying treasure up for the "sweet by and by." No, it means that your heavenly account is charged, and you can make withdrawals here on earth. But, the "forsaking all" aspect is real. You must be truly willing. This brings us to the next criterion for being a true disciple.

5. True Disciples Forsake All.

Continuing from the last example, in the Scripture, Jesus invites several men to become disciples by simply saying, "Follow Me." In some cases, Jesus asks them to quit their jobs (Matt. 4:19; 9:9), in another He says to let the dead bury their own dead (Matt. 8:22), but to the rich young ruler, He says,

> *"If you want to be perfect, go, sell what you have and give to the poor, and you will have treasure in heaven; and come, follow Me."*

> Matthew 19:21

In order for this young man to be perfect, Jesus tells him to sell what he has and give to the poor. Jesus does not ask His other disciples to sell all their possessions—although there is always something to forsake and leave behind.

The rich young ruler is not willing, and he leaves feeling sorrowful because he does not want to part with his great wealth. Jesus knows this young man has a problem concerning his possessions; they are idols to him.

Jesus is sad when the young man does not accept His offer. Jesus loves him, and He wants to make an exchange with him and give him treasures in heaven. Let me tell you, heaven is a whole lot better off than the earth—no banks, no debt, and they use gold to pave the streets.

> *You must realize that you cannot out give the Lord.*

You must realize that you cannot out give the Lord. Yet, people want to ignore that. They say, "If I'm a true disciple, Jesus will want everything I have!" Well, He gave you everything you have anyway. It is already His. If He tells you to return it, then it is good seed sown. Give it gladly. Do not have the same problem as this rich young ruler. GIVE!

As a follower of Jesus, you want to forsake all to be a true disciple. Then, when you are one of His true disciples, BLESSED ARE YOU!

True Disciples Walk in the Blessing

When you are a true disciple, then the blessings are with you. Such is the focus of Jesus' teaching to His disciples in Matthew 5:3-12. He teaches what you can expect when you are a TRUE DISCIPLE.

CHAPTER 3

JESUS TEACHES HIS DISCIPLES

Throughout the Scriptures, Jesus goes about preaching the good news of the Gospel. However, on one very important occasion, Jesus removes Himself from the multitudes to teach His disciples exclusively. The necessity of this message is to equip His disciples to spread the Gospel in a Christ-like manner and to walk in the blessing.

Often referred to as the Sermon on the Mount, Matthew chapters 5, 6, and 7 comprise one continuous teaching by Jesus to His disciples concerning how to deal with the issues of life. However, Jesus is not speaking to all Christians. This is established at the beginning of the teaching when Jesus' disciples come to Him and He teaches them in Matthew 5:1:

> *And seeing the multitudes, He went up on a mountain, and when He was seated His **disciples** came to Him.*

Notice the whole multitude did not come to Him. And by disciples, it does not mean just the twelve apostles. Continuing with verse 2:

> *Then He opened His mouth and taught them* [the disciples], *saying.*

The subject of the next ten verses is Jesus speaking about walking in the blessing. The fact that He addresses the blessings first reveals their importance. He begins by teaching His disciples how to walk in the blessing when faced with the issues of life (remember, the blessing flowing from your born-again spirit acts as a hedge of protection). In order to be effective and remain in the blessing, you must maintain a Christian character, no matter what the issues may be.

Jesus promises His disciples they will be blessed if they adhere to His teaching in nine specific areas. Often called the Beatitudes, I contend that these are not random "attitudes that should be" put forth by Jesus in order to be blessed. Rather, He is saying, "As true disciples, I want you to be blessed. Here are the spiritual forces that must flow through your life so that the issues, circumstances, and situations of life will not overcome you."

Jesus does not leave us in the dark concerning the issues of life. I do not know about you, but I am a disciple. I am here to learn, follow the teachings, and say what Jesus taught me to say. I wish to imitate my Teacher and abide in His Word.

If you are a follower of Jesus, you want to do what it takes to be a true disciple. First and foremost, watch your thought life and what you are feeding your heart because that is what will flow out of you (Prov. 4:23). It always flows out of your mouth and your actions.

And the tongue is a fire, a world of iniquity. The tongue is so set among our members that it defiles the whole body, and sets on fire the course of nature; and it is set on fire by hell.

James 3:6

29

As a man thinks in his heart, so is he.

Now recall Proverbs 23:7, which states that as a man thinks in his heart, so is he. If not guarded by the Word of God, what you think about to the point that it drops into your heart becomes who you really are. As a result, what you have meditated and pondered on are the issues that flow out of your heart and set on fire the course of your life. That is why the Word says to guard your heart and watch over it because not only are the issues of your life determined, but so is your character.

With the nine pronounced blessings of Matthew 5:3-12, Jesus teaches His disciples how to walk with godly character. Throughout the Scriptures, Jesus Himself embodies all of these characteristics:

"Blessed are the poor in spirit, for theirs is the kingdom of heaven.

"Blessed are those who mourn, for they shall be comforted.

"Blessed are the meek, for they shall inherit the earth.

"Blessed are those who hunger and thirst for righteousness, for they shall be filled.

"Blessed are the merciful, for they shall obtain mercy.

"Blessed are the pure in heart, for they shall see God.

"Blessed are the peacemakers, for they shall be called sons of God.

"Blessed are those who are persecuted for right-eousness' sake, for theirs is the kingdom of heaven.

"Blessed are you when they revile and persecute you, and say all kinds of evil against you falsely for My sake. Rejoice and be exceedingly glad, for great is your reward in heaven, for so they persecuted the prophets who were before you."

Matthew 5:3-12

The subject of Jesus' message is easy to determine. It is HOW TO BE BLESSED! How to walk in the blessing when the issues of life come your way. Nine times in these Scriptures Jesus says, "Blessed are you." If Jesus says you are blessed, then you are and will continue to be more blessed, and that blessing comes from developing the character of a true disciple.

For example, my mental capacity continues to increase. Not because I am so smart, but because my mind continues to be blessed and more blessed.

In this passage, many want to focus on the words "poor," "mourn," "meek," and "hunger," but why not focus on the word "blessed"?

When we get to heaven, we will no longer need to walk in the blessing—there is no mourning, for instance, in heaven. The purpose of walking in the blessing is for the here and now! As a true disciple, when dealing with the everyday issues of life, whether you feel like it or not, Jesus calls you blessed.

Why Focus on the Blessing?

You may think, "Why deal so much with the blessing?"

In Genesis chapter 1, God made man and saw that everything was very good. Then, He blessed man and gave him dominion and authority to replenish and multiply. God gave the blessing for us to use in this earth in the Garden of Eden.

Through sin, Babylon took over, which has now translated into the world's system. HOWEVER, when sin was introduced into the earth, it DID NOT remove God's will for the creation of man to be blessed. **God desires to bless you.**

Why does God desire this? Let me show you. If you are having trouble with this reality, you need to get it settled. I sometimes ask my congregation to say aloud, "I'm Blessed." I am amazed to see how many people look as though they have trouble saying that. You should be shouting it aloud so that the thought will get into your heart and set the course in your life.

God Desires to Bless You

In Matthew 5:3-12, Jesus gives nine pronounced blessings to His disciples. And we know through the Scriptures that Jesus only does what He sees His Father doing.

> *"Most assuredly, I say to you, the Son can do nothing of Himself, but what He sees the Father do; for whatever He does, the Son also does in like manner.*

> John 5:19

Therefore, we know Jesus would not have given promised blessings on His own. He had to hear them from His heavenly Father, which means it is God's will for us to be blessed.

God is Blessed!

In addition to it being God's will for you to be blessed, being blessed is one of God's characteristics. **Blessed is who He is!**

Would you agree that God is pretty blessed? He paves His streets with gold. Gold is just pavement to Him. He uses pearls for gates. Have you ever thought about the size of that oyster? How big would it have to be? And you and I have dominion over that sucker. That is authority!

*According to the glorious gospel of the **blessed** God which was committed to my trust.*

I Timothy 1:11

God is a blessed God.

Have you ever noticed a parent's face when their child receives a blessing? Sometimes they are more excited than the child. How much more then would our heavenly Father want to see us blessed (Luke 11:13).

*Which He will manifest in His own time, He who is the **blessed** and only Potentate, the King of kings and Lord of lords.*

I Timothy 6:15

God wants you blessed because He is blessed. In fact, the same Greek word *makarios* is used to describe our blessed God in the Scriptures we just read and the blessings of the true disciples in Matthew 5:3-11. What that means is that God wants you, as true disciples, to be blessed in the same manner that He is blessed. Further, it is His will and His character for you to be blessed, and we are made in His image and likeness (Gen. 1:26).

> *Being blessed is a characteristic that flows from your reborn spirit.*

That is why Jesus says "blessed, blessed, blessed are you." He did not even focus on the curse, curse, curse. He simply laid out the blessings to walk in when you face the everyday issues of life.

When you see "blessed" as a characteristic on the *inside of you* rather than something that may or may not *come upon you*, you will not be moved by external circumstances. Being blessed is a characteristic that flows from your reborn spirit that allows you to walk through worldly issues.

"Blessed" is Present Tense

In the Greek, when the word *blessed* is used as a verb (something you do) or an adjective (something that describes), it sounds like something in the past tense: has blessed or been blessed. However, the Greek rendering is not speaking of a past or future tense—it actually means "right now." Therefore, when Jesus says "Blessed," He is not talking about a blessing that is going to come upon you in the future. He is talking about a blessing that you can walk in RIGHT NOW because it will flow out of you.

Jesus is saying to you and me, as His true disciples, that "blessed" should manifest in our lives all of the time; it is not something in the past or future, but now. "BLESSED is he who mourns . . ." Blessed becomes part of your character.

Definition of Blessed

The word *blessed* in the Greek is *makarios,* which means "to be happy" and "to enjoy enviable favor." Do not get stuck on the word *enviable.* It is not a negative word in this sense.

Matthew 5:3 in the *Amplified Bible* reads:

> *Blessed (happy, to be envied, and spiritually prosperous—with life-joy and satisfaction in God's favor and salvation, regardless of their outward conditions) are the poor in spirit . . .*

So, if you are blessed, then you are happy, enjoying enviable favor, and spiritually prosperous, regardless of outward conditions.

I do not know about you, but I know I have favor—particularly God's favor. But, enviable favor means someone else sees favor in your life, and they desire it in an enviable way.

Enjoying enviable favor is a positive thing. People should look at you and say, "Wow, I don't know what it is, but that person is enjoying life, happy, spiritually strong, and prospering with favor. I need to find out what they have because I want some of it!"

If you are a true disciple, then you are walking in the same characteristics as those people Jesus is talking to on the mountain—His disciples. Others will see your success and happiness, and they will want to walk like you do.

Blessed Means Success

While we have examined the word *blessed* used to describe the character of a true disciple, the word *blessed* also comes from the Greek word *eulogeo*, which is an action word that indicates a blessing is bestowed. In this case, the word *blessed* means "to cause to be happy" and "empowered to prosper." By being blessed, God is saying that He will not only cause you to be happy, but He will empower you to prosper in the things He has asked you to do. Wow! That is reassurance! That is how you succeed!

CHAPTER 4

SPIRITUAL
PROGRESSION

As we have discovered, the Sermon on the Mount is not really a sermon, but Jesus teaching His true disciples (you and me) concerning the issues of life. Jesus removes Himself from the multitudes, and His disciples come to Him. Everywhere else Jesus goes, He is preaching the kingdom of God, but on this occasion, Jesus teaches His true disciples about how to deal with the issues of life.

The beginning portion, called the Beatitudes, is Jesus teaching His disciples how to walk in the blessing even though the issues of life are all around them. Not merely attitudes, Jesus instructs on how to maintain a Christian *character* no matter what the issues are. This is how you walk in the blessing.

Jesus is not just randomly throwing out thoughts under the anointing, but laying out a progression.

On first read, you might believe what Jesus teaches in Matthew 5:3-12 to be individual, stand-alone issues a disciple will face. However, there is something in the Scriptures called a **spiritual progression**. In these verses, Jesus is not just randomly throwing out thoughts under the anointing, but laying out a progression. An example of another spiritual progression in the Bible is found in John 10:10.

*"The thief does not come except to **steal**, and to **kill**, and to **destroy**. I have come that they may have life, and that they may have it more abundantly."*

John 10:10

The progression is (1) steal, (2) then kill, (3) then destroy. It is a flow, a spiritual progression, because the next part says, *"I have come that they may have life, and that they may have it more abundantly."*

Jesus is saying, "The thief comes to steal, kill, and destroy [a progression], but I have come so they may have life, and have it more abundantly [a progression]."[1]

The same is true with the development of godly character in Matthew 5:3-12. Jesus is purposeful in the order of their progression. He is talking about a spiritual progression that must take place in order for you to deal with the issues of life effectively, develop your character, and walk in the blessing. It is how you will progress as a true disciple. While we will deal with each of these characteristics in more detail in the Chapters to follow, the following is an overview of that progression.

Spiritual Progression Toward God

The first four characteristics of a true disciple deal with developing a relationship with God, with a progression moving toward God. This progression is found in verses 3-6. Jesus says,

> *3 "Blessed are the poor in spirit, for theirs is the kingdom of heaven."*

---

[1] For more study concerning the spiritual progression found in John 10:10, read my book entitled *The Way of Cain.*

4 "Blessed are those who mourn, for they shall be comforted."

5 "Blessed are the meek, for they shall inherit the earth."

6 "Blessed are those who hunger and thirst for righteousness, for they shall be filled."

In this first progression, you will (1) become poor in spirit, (2) then mourn, (3) then become meek. As you progress through these three stages, you build a relationship with God, and these characteristics will flow out of your heart, or reborn spirit, in everything you face. You are moving toward God, while at the same time walking in the blessing through the issues of life. Because Jesus says that you are blessed when your character develops in this way, the result of that progression is (4) you will hunger and thirst for righteousness.

So, in the presence of God, after you have become (1) poor in spirit, (2) mournful, and (3) meek, then you will (4) hunger and thirst for righteousness. When you reach the hungering and thirsting for righteousness phase, the Scripture says "you shall be filled."

We know we want to deal with the issues of life effectively, develop our character, and walk in the blessing. HOWEVER, such benefits will only **progress** through being poor in spirit, mourning, meekness, and hungering and thirsting for righteousness. After those four characteristics are fulfilled in you, you are prepared for the next spiritual progression.

Spiritual Progression Toward Man

After you are filled, the next progression is building a relationship toward man. This progression is found in verses 7-10. Jesus says,

> 7 *"Blessed are the merciful, for they shall obtain mercy."*
>
> 8 *"Blessed are the pure in heart, for they shall see God."*
>
> 9 *"Blessed are the peacemakers, for they shall be called sons of God."*
>
> 10 *"Blessed are those who are persecuted for righteousness' sake, for theirs is the kingdom of heaven."*

This spiritual progression concerns how to deal with others and *their* issues of life. After you have been filled in the presence of God through the first progression, you become (5) merciful, (6) then pure in heart, (7) then a peacemaker, and (8) then you will be persecuted for righteousness' sake.

When you progress through all eight stages, you will reach the ninth and final stage of the progression, which is described in verses 11 and 12:

> *"Blessed are you when they revile and persecute you, and say all kinds of evil against you falsely for My sake. Rejoice and be exceedingly glad, for great is*

your reward in heaven, for so they persecuted the prophets who were before you."

When you reach the ninth stage, get prepared, because people will say all sorts of evil things about you. In the face of this persecution, Jesus says to REJOICE because not only are you blessed in the here and now, but great is your reward in heaven!

You build your relationship and character in your daily walk toward God first.

So, you build your relationship and character in your daily walk toward God first, then you come out full. Now you direct that fullness toward man, and you deal mercifully, you deal in pureness of heart, and you deal as a peacemaker. As you deal properly in these areas, Jesus says that you will suffer persecution.

Two Reasons for Persecution

The eighth and ninth spiritual progression both indicate that you will be persecuted, but it is for two different reasons. The first will bring persecution for righteousness' sake. Unfortunately, much of this persecution will come from other Christians.

Any time you dedicate yourself to become a true disciple, Jesus says the result is persecution for righteousness' sake. If you have yet to experience this for yourself, I am saddened to tell you that no one can gossip, pick on you, or be meaner to you than other Christians.

Have you ever been an object of other Christians picking on you and saying ugly things about you? The truth of the matter had no bearing on the issue, right? If your answer is no, then, bless your heart, you must not get out at all! Because anytime you start conducting yourself like a disciple, Jesus says the result is persecution for righteousness' sake.

But, that is not the last one.

Verse 11 says, *"Blessed are you when they revile and persecute you, and say all kinds of evil against you falsely for My sake."*

In this verse, Jesus is speaking of the world persecuting you for His sake. You might say, "Why would I want to have this kind of blessed character if the result is the world hating me?" Well, Jesus says you are not of the world, and the world should hate you.

> *"If you were of the world, the world would love its own. Yet because you are not of the world, but I chose you out of the world, therefore the world hates you."*
>
> John 15:19

In fact, if the world **does not** hate you, what does that say about you as a Christian? Does the world even see a difference?

When you reach this ninth, and last, stage in the spiritual progression, it is the result of walking in the first eight characteristics. When people say evil and false things about you because you are a true disciple of Jesus Christ, you have completed the progression. AND YOU ARE BLESSED!

Characteristics of True Disciples

The character of the blessed comprises those characteristics possessed by true disciples while dealing with the issues of life. The following is a review of what has been revealed through the Scriptures:

As a true disciple in the presence of God, if you will be:

1. Poor in spirit,

2. Mournful, and

3. Meek.

Then you will:

4. Hunger and thirst for righteousness and be filled.

Once you are filled, then you will pour out that filling to the world by becoming:

5. Merciful,

6. Pure in heart,

7. Peacemaker,

8. And then persecuted for righteousness' sake.

When you have those eight moving in your life, I can tell you right now, you are going to have the ninth one rear its ugly head up.

9. You are persecuted for Jesus' sake.

But, what does Jesus say?

"BLESSED ARE YOU when they revile and persecute you, and say all kinds of evil against you falsely for My sake. Rejoice and be exceedingly glad, for GREAT IS YOUR REWARD IN HEAVEN, for so they persecuted the prophets who were before you."

In other words, Jesus is saying, "Let me give you this warning up front. The world will revile and persecute you, and say all kinds of evil against you falsely, but take heart, it is because of Me."

As a pastor, I desire for everyone to walk as a true disciple and in the blessing. But, make no mistake, when you get these first eight done (and if you have already done so, you know what I am talking about), the ninth one will rear its ugly head because God blesses you as you walk in the blessing, and the world hates you for it.

Now that you understand that these godly characteristics are a progression, we will look at each one in greater detail.

CHAPTER 5

BLESSED ARE THE POOR IN SPIRIT

Blessed are the poor in spirit,
for theirs is the kingdom of heaven.

—Matthew 5:3

At the beginning of Matthew chapter 5, we find Jesus seated on a mountain with His disciples around Him. Jesus begins teaching them how to walk blessed as they develop the character of a true disciple. His instructions are concise, yet rich with understanding and wisdom. He lays out a spiritual progression that will ensure success and blessings for His disciples as they face the issues of life. The progression begins with being *poor in spirit.*

What does it mean to be *poor in spirit?*

The *Amplified Bible* reads:

*Blessed (happy, to be envied, and spiritually prosperous—with life-joy and satisfaction in God's favor and salvation, regardless of their outward conditions) are the poor in spirit **(the humble, who rate themselves insignificant)**, for theirs is the kingdom of heaven!*

This translation reveals the *poor in spirit* are humble, and they rate themselves insignificant. Notice it does not say that God rates them insignificant, nor does it say that they ARE insignificant. It says they rate THEMSELVES insignificant. But, this does not mean they are monetarily poor.

A number of Christian denominations and religions focus solely on the "poor" part, but leave off the "in spirit."

They say, "Blessed are the **poor**, for theirs is the kingdom of heaven."

Being poor, as in having no money, is not a criterion for a blessing.

The Word does not say that at all. In fact, I know numerous poor people who are absolutely NOT blessed. Being poor, as in having no money, is not a criterion for a blessing. Please do not think in that way. Such is a poverty mentality, and it will not bless you. You must renew your mind.

It is a purely "religious" idea to believe that if you own nothing, give everything away, and struggle through life to pay your bills that you will be blessed because you have riches in heaven. That is a theology we discussed previously called *asceticism*, and it is not Bible.

Jesus says, *"Blessed* [happy, to be envied, and spiritually prosperous] *are the poor in **spirit**, for theirs is the kingdom of heaven."* This blessing has nothing to do with your financial situation.

I believe the *Contemporary English Version* has the most accurate Greek rendering of *poor in spirit*. It reads:

God blesses those people who depend only on him. They belong to the kingdom of heaven.

In the Greek, the phrase *poor in spirit* actually refers to a spiritual state. It is a godly humility wherein you know everything you have and everything you are is dependent upon God. That is what being spiritually poor means.

The word *poor* in the Greek is *ptochos*, which means "a shrinking from something" or "to cringe like a beggar." It is an individual so poor that they depend on another's mercy from an outside source. Further, the actual root word for *mercy* in Hebrew is *hesed*, which means "God has an overwhelming desire to do you good," which is the blessing.

Therefore, being **poor in spirit** is not referring to one's financial or physical condition. Someone poor in spirit is a person who depends totally and completely on God's overwhelming desire to do them good. It does not mean to be beaten down, spiritually weak, a lack of faith, or going through afflictions, trials, and temptations. We know that "*we are more than conquerors through Him who loved us*" (Rom. 8:37).

Poor in spirit also means "to be empty or void of reality" and "helpless to save oneself."

It is not by accident that Jesus started with poor in spirit in a disciple's spiritual progression. In order to walk effectively through the issues of life, you must become empty and void. In other words, you have to empty yourself of your ego and realize that it is God's mercy that provides for your advancement and effectiveness. *Poor in spirit* means to "empty oneself."

In fact, it is the only instruction that begins with "emptying." The other instructions concern either God filling you or you pouring yourself out to others. Being poor in spirit is nothing more than doing what Jesus did, which is to say,

> *"I can of Myself do nothing . . . because I do not seek My own will but the will of the Father who sent Me."*

John 5:30

This means all you have, all you do, and everywhere you walk is the manifestation of God in you.

The Almighty Ego

One of biggest enemies to walking in the blessing is one's ego. We are faith people, yes, but we need to understand everything we have comes because of Him. Such is the beginning of a disciple's progression—being poor in spirit.

As you walk closer to Him, the more spiritually strong you will become—and the more spiritually strong you become, the more you realize it is not you, but Him working in you. It is *"Christ in you, the hope of glory"* (Col. 1:27, KJV). To be poor in spirit is to be spiritually dependent on the Lord. Not independent.

We live in an independent society. Many say, "I'll do my own thing." Such an attitude is prevalent, even in the Body of Christ. If you want to get people mad, just touch their independence.

If you believe you can do things yourself without God, then that is pride.

People are going to be surprised when they get to heaven. It is not a democracy; it is a theocracy, and there is no arguing over who "Theo" is. It is God, and that is it. Just try to bring yourself against heaven's system; you will find out what Satan discovered, which is how quickly you can be cast down. Such an attitude is PRIDE!

Watch Out For Pride

Pride is another huge hindrance to being poor in spirit. The Word says,

> *So humble yourselves under the mighty power of God, and at the right time he will lift you up in honor. Give all your worries and cares to God, for he cares about you.*

I Peter 5:6-7, NLT

No matter how strong you become spiritually, walking in the blessing through everyday issues will make you more dependent on God, not more independent. If you believe you can do things yourself without God, then that is pride.

Dependence on the World's System

Probably the biggest danger in our society is depending on the flesh instead of God. Having confidence in the flesh is having confidence in the world's system, which is the metamorphosis of the Babylonian system. Idol worship originated in ancient Babylon.

When your dependency is in the world's system, you are in trouble. For example, we live in a society where so many people are dependent on the government. Of course, we should help the poor and needy, and we need to reach out to people who have needs—that is Bible; however, our *dependency* should never be on unions, jobs, or the government. When such is the case, it is idolatry. No matter what excuses you come up with to convince yourself otherwise, when your source and what you depend on is anything other than God, then you are in idolatry.

Dependency on anything other than God is the *opposite* of being poor in spirit.

Whether you like me or not, I am going to tell you the truth. I am not writing this book to win a popularity contest. You are to be dependent spiritually on Jesus, the Father, and the Holy Spirit only.

In fact, the government should never have been in the business of helping people. Scripturally, that is the job of the Church. We have a commandment to help the poor, widows, orphans, needy, and those in prisons (Matt. 25:36). Although such assistance should come through the Body of Christ, even most churches have allowed, and expect, the government to take over this role. Yet, the government's involvement in benevolence forces recipients to become dependent upon them, not God.

True disciples are to be spiritually dependent upon God, meaning you can do nothing of yourself; thereby, being without ego, pride, or dependence upon the world's system. Such is being poor in spirit.

Becoming Spiritually Dependent

For some people, the term *poor in spirit* does not resonate with them; they have difficultly wrapping their minds around it, or they just do not like the word *poor*. Instead, we can use the term *spiritually dependent*. It means the same thing.

When you are faced with the decision to become spiritually dependent, most people will respond one of four ways.

1. Deny it.

If you believe anything you have is because of you, you are in denial. When faced with the decision to become spiritually dependent on God, most people will deny the need to do so. This will cause one to become deceived, and then self-deceived by trying to justify their position. Self-deception is the most powerful deception that exists.

In fact, if you believe you have any good thing right now because of you, whether it is a great job, family, or possessions, then you are sadly in the dark. Everything you have is because of the Lord and Him only. It is His overwhelming desire to do you good that brings about the good life you know.

2. Admit it—then attempt change in your own power.

The second response is to admit the need to become spiritually dependent on God, but then attempt to achieve that dependence in your own power. That does not even make sense, does it? Depending on yourself to become dependent on God? No, and it does not work either.

Why do you think the self-help fad has been so popular? Because people want to help themselves, by themselves. This fad has even crept into churches and Christian circles. I am not saying that you do not need help, but self-help is not the answer to becoming spiritually dependent on God. You can admit the need, but the only way to actually BECOME poor in spirit, according to the Word, is by **self-denial**. The key is self-denial, not self-help.

The first step to self-denial is to realize you **cannot help yourself**, and that you are spiritually dependent on Him. So say, "Father, I repent. I admit it. I cast my care over on You, Lord. I humble myself before You. I have been into pride, idolatry, and self-deception, and I want You to cause me to be blessed in life by being dependent only on You."

3. Admit it—then give up in despair.

The third response is to admit the need to become spiritually dependent on God, but instead of moving forward in that knowledge, sink into depression or despair, and just give up.

As we can see, simply admitting the need to become spiritually dependent is not the answer. We have seen two scenarios where someone admits the need, but either tries to improve in their own strength, or simply gives up. Once you admit the need, you still have to do something about it.

4. Admit it—then turn to God for help.

Jesus says, "Blessed are those who spiritually depend on God, for theirs is the kingdom of heaven." Poor in spirit is being spiritually dependent on God in every area.

Poor in spirit is being spiritually dependent on God in every area.

As you become poor in spirit, you begin to empty yourself. It gets YOU out of the way so that Christ can develop a character in you that causes you to be blessed when you face adverse conditions in the world. It is relying on God for EVERYTHING.

It is the first in the spiritual progression that says, "God, I can do nothing without You. I want to live, breathe, have my very being in You and obtain Your mercy. As I empty myself of self, and make myself available for You to use, I ask that You anoint me, flow through me, and allow me to be a blessing in the issues of life."

Blessed are the Poor in Spirit

Jesus says, *"Blessed* [happy, to be envied, and spiritually prosperous] *are the poor in spirit* [being spiritually dependent on God with no ego or pride, and casting your care over on Him], *for theirs is the kingdom of heaven."*

Jesus promises that if you become spiritually dependent on God, then yours is the kingdom of heaven. The word *kingdom* in the Greek is *basileia*, which means "sovereignty, royal power, dominion." To belong to the kingdom of heaven means to walk in dominion as you face the issues of life as one who is royalty. That is part of what the blessing of enviable favor is all about. People will notice that you walk around with the anointing and favor of one in the Royal Family, and Jesus is our King!

It starts by emptying yourself in the presence of God and realizing you can do nothing without Him. Once there, you find yourself at the next stage: *the blessing that comes through mourning.*

CHAPTER 6

BLESSED ARE THOSE WHO MOURN

*B*LESSED ARE THOSE WHO MOURN,

FOR THEY SHALL BE COMFORTED.

—*MATTHEW 5:4*

As we continue our study concerning the development of godly character, Jesus is teaching His disciples how to deal with the issues of life and walk in the blessing. For this development to occur, Jesus says that we must walk out a spiritual progression toward God.

The first step in this progression is *poor in spirit*, which is emptying ourselves before God and becoming completely dependent on Him for everything. Once this occurs, you will find the next phase, which is **mourning**. In this instance, to *mourn* means "godly sorrow."

Godly Sorrow is Not Grief

Do not let the word *mourn* mislead you. It does not mean "grief." There is no such thing as "good grief." Grief is designed to overwhelm you and kill you, and it is Satan's counterfeit to godly sorrow. Grief is a worldly sorrow, and worldly sorrows lead to death (II Cor. 7:10).

Grief cannot bless you.

You can be sorrowful and have sadness, but that is not the same as grief. For example, if someone loses a loved one, that person can grieve to the point they become useless to anyone around them. Grief will debilitate you, and it is not from God. Grief cannot bless you, and it is not what Jesus is talking about. *"Blessed are those who mourn"* is not "blessed are those who grieve," although some have tried to translate it that way.

The *Amplified Bible* reads:

> *Blessed and enviably happy [with a happiness produced by the experience of God's favor and especially conditioned by the revelation of His matchless grace] are those who mourn, for they shall be comforted!*

The Message, which is a Bible commentary, not a translation, says:

> *"You're blessed when you feel you've lost what is most dear to you. Only then can you be embraced by the One most dear to you."*

This passage says that when you lose what is MOST dear to you, then you can be comforted by the ONE most dear. In other words, once you have emptied yourself (by being spiritually dependent on the Lord), there is a mourning (godly sorrow) that takes place and starts its proper work in you.

Definition of Mourning

The word *mourn* in the Greek is *pentheo*, which means "to lament over the dead." However, if you go to *Vine's* and other Bible dictionaries, *pentheo* has several definitions.

First, it means "to be sorrowful over the death of a loved one." An example of this usage is in Mark 16:10:

She went and told those who had been with Him, as they mourned and wept.

Second, it means "to be sorrowful over a serious and painful loss of something." An example of this usage is when the world mourns the overthrow of the Babylonian system (the current world's system) during the Tribulation Period:

"And the merchants of the earth will weep and mourn over her, for no one buys their merchandise anymore . . . the merchants of these things, who became rich by her, will stand at a distance for fear of her torment, weeping and wailing."

Revelation 18:11, 15

Yet, the definition that most closely relates to Matthew 5:4 and the spiritual progression associated with Jesus' teaching is "to be sorrowful for sin or for condoning it." The following verses are examples of the word *mourn* used in this sense:

Lament and mourn and weep! Let your laughter be turned to mourning and your joy to gloom.

James 4:9

And you are puffed up, and have not rather mourned, that he who has done this deed might be taken away from among you.

I Corinthians 5:2

As in Matthew 5:4, these verses use *mourn* in the sense "to be sorrowful over sin or the condoning of sin." In the spiritual progression, once you become poor in spirit, you will begin to mourn and lament over sin.

I am amazed at the number of people in the Body of Christ who are not mournful over the sin and rebellion that is running rampant in the world. In fact, there are some churches that are embracing this sin and changing their theology to condone it further! Instead, there should be mourning and lamenting over that sin. Not only for the sin in the world, but over those who condone the sin. I am not saying that you should confront the sinner in all cases, but you should be sorry over the sin.

Yet, we live in a society that has almost become calloused to sin. Jesus says, "Blessed are those who are spiritually dependent because they rely on the power of God to cause the kingdom to work in their lives. It is they who will mourn over the sin that is going on around them."

Godly Sorrow Unto Repentance

In First Corinthians chapter 5, the apostle Paul writes a letter to the Corinthian church concerning an issue of sexual immorality within its congregation. Specifically, a young man and his stepmother are involved in incest, yet they continue to go to church without any correction.

Concerning this couple, Paul writes, *"Deliver such a one to Satan for the destruction of the flesh, that his spirit may be saved in the day of the Lord Jesus"* (I Cor. 5:5). Here, Paul instructs the church to separate themselves from this couple to allow for repentance and saving of the soul.

Later, when the young man repents and wants to come back, the church does not allow him to return. They continue to hold his sin against him. For this reason, Paul writes a second letter to straighten them out. He tells them that they were right to distain the sin; HOWEVER, they must allow for repentance and restoration. The church listens to Paul and repents.

For godly sorrow produces repentance leading to salvation, not to be regretted; but the sorrow of the world produces death.

For observe this very thing, that you sorrowed in a godly manner: What diligence it produced in you, what clearing of yourselves, what indignation, what fear, what vehement desire, what zeal, what vindication! In all things you proved yourselves to be clear in this matter.

II Corinthians 7:10-11

> **Godly sorrow works unto repentance.**

Did you notice that true, godly sorrow leads to repentance and produces a clearing and reverential fear of God? Godly sorrow makes a change in you which causes you to be diligent. It causes you to be clear. It has a power!

Since the church in Corinth produced a godly sorrow unto repentance, they changed their approach in dealing with sin. Godly sorrow works unto repentance. Worldly sorrow, such as grief, works unto death. You are blessed when you mourn over sin, but the purpose of that mourning has to be restoration and mercy.

Biblical Reasons for Mourning

Jesus tells us that we are blessed for mourning with a godly sorrow. The following are biblical reasons for this type of mourning.

1. Losing Fellowship with the Father.

The first biblical reason for mourning is realizing the severe loss of losing fellowship with God because of sin. To be in sin or condone sin causes you to lose your fellowship and closeness with the Lord.

Have you ever looked back in your life and realized, "Man, if I hadn't done that, where would I be today?" Or, "If I had known ten years ago what I know now, how much closer my relationship would be with the Lord."

When you see how severely you have messed up your relationship with the Father because of sin or a bad choice, there is mourning that occurs. You recognize how severe it was to be separated from the Blesser, and you realize, with a godly sorrow, all the time and blessings you have missed. That is why Jesus says, "Blessed are those who mourn," because it is mourning unto repentance, and a resolve to never lose fellowship again.

2. Poor Performance.

A second reason to mourn is because of present and continuous poor performance. There are many people who perform poorly, and because of that, they mourn.

I know people who have settled for poor performance. However, in their minds, they think they are doing great because they are narcissists. Politicians are an excellent example of this. Of course, I am not referring to all politicians, but most actually believe they are doing great in their poor performance.

For a true disciple, when you realize you have been performing poorly, it causes you to mourn with a godly sorrow. Maybe you are not faithful with your tithe? Maybe you are always late to church or work? Maybe you gossip? Maybe you are fearful? Maybe you do not always tell the truth—or something else? All of these are examples of poor performance that, once exposed, will cause a true disciple to mourn for falling short. However, you are not supposed to stay that way. Once the Holy Spirit reveals an area of poor performance, you must make a change for the better.

How about making a mistake? Poor performance in this area will cause a true disciple to feel sorry, primarily because God knows. Even if the mistake is not intentional, there is still a sorrow because God is aware of it.

Now, I am not talking about getting caught doing something wrong by another person. You can be a spiritual knot on a log and realize anyone can be sorry when they are caught. That is why if someone in a relationship gets caught doing something wrong, it takes a while for that relationship to heal— even if there is an apology. Why? Because the repentance did not come before the person was caught.

How many are genuinely sorrowful BEFORE being caught doing something wrong? Just because you were not caught in the act of something, does not mean that God did not catch you. God knew it. He probably sent things across your path to help steer you clear of it, but you ignored them. That is why it is such an abomination to cry out, "God, why did You let this happen?" He probably sent several warning flares to help you avoid a certain thing, but you did it anyway.

Forget anyone else knowing. If you feel sorry just because God knows, then that is godly sorrow. And it is godly sorrow unto repentance, not self-condemnation. You do not need to dwell on it once you have repented and changed your course. I know a lot of people who beat themselves up over mistakes they have made, and that is not godly sorrow; neither is self-pity or depression.

You mourn because of your poor performance. However, once you recognize poor performance in an area, do not stay that way. Repent, and correct that behavior. Of course, make sure it is the sin you are mourning over, and not the consequences of sin.

3. World's Sin.

The sin of the world is another biblical reason for mourning. As the Body of Christ, the amount of sin and rebellion in the world should make us sorrowful.

4. Shallowness of the Church.

A final reason for mourning with godly sorrow is because of the shallowness of the Church. Peter writes:

> *For if God spared not the angels that sinned, but cast them down to hell, and delivered them into chains of darkness, to be reserved unto judgment; and spared not the old world, but saved Noah the eighth person, a preacher of righteousness, bringing in the flood upon the world of the ungodly; and turning the cities of Sodom and Gomorrha into ashes condemned them with an overthrow, making them an ensample unto those that after should live ungodly; and delivered just Lot, vexed with the filthy conversation of the wicked:* **(For that righteous man dwelling among them, in seeing and hearing, vexed his righteous soul from day to day with their unlawful deeds.)**
>
> *The Lord knoweth how to deliver the godly out of temptations, and to reserve the unjust unto the day of judgment to be punished.*
>
> II Peter 2:4-9, KJV

What Peter is saying is that you and I should be sorrowful over the present shallowness of the Church—particularly those of us who are filled with the Holy Spirit and have empowerment to do the works of Jesus. The Church is considered shallow when it depends on the arm of the flesh instead of the Holy Spirit and the anointing.

The Church also reveals shallowness in the acceptance of sin in our ministers. Yes, we have to walk in love, but we are supposed to feel godly sorrow when there is sin separating fellowship with God.

And When You Sorrow . . .

There is a promise that comes with every instance of godly sorrow, whether it is for mourning over the world's sin, the condoning of sin, or the sin that leads to repentance. Jesus says, **"YOU SHALL BE COMFORTED."**

CHAPTER 7

BLESSED ARE THE MEEK

Blessed are the meek,
for they shall inherit the earth.
—Matthew 5:5

After you become spiritually dependent on God (poor in spirit), and you mourn with a godly sorrow over sin, your spiritual progression will lead you to **meekness**.

Probably one of the most misunderstood words in our society, and in the Greek, is the word *meek*.

The *New Living Translation* uses the word *humble*.

*God blesses those who are **humble**, for they will inherit the whole earth.*

The *New Jerusalem Bible* uses the word *gentle*.

*Blessed are the **gentle**: they shall have the earth as inheritance.*

> *Probably one of the most misunderstood words in our society is the word meek.*

The words *meek*, *humble*, and *gentle* are all translated from the same Greek word *praus*. The use of the word *meek* in Matthew 5:5 comes from *praus* in an adjective form, which means "gentle, mild, and humble." However, *praus* also means "a gentle, soothing disposition."

Therefore, to be meek is to be of a soothing disposition. Jesus is saying,

"Blessed are those who have a soothing disposition, for they shall inherit the earth." Wow, that sounds nice, and very spiritually progressed!

True Disciples Have a Soothing Disposition

Let me ask you, has it ever been said of you that you have a *soothing disposition* when faced with the issues of life and the conditions going on around you?

I believe it is safe to say that no one has ever said that about me as of yet. Unfortunately, having a soothing disposition under pressure cannot be attributed to most people. It is more like, "Whoa, back off and get away from him, he is going through something." Such is the *opposite* of meekness.

Let us look at another translation of the word *meek*.

The noun form of meekness in the Greek is *prautes*, which means "that temper of spirit in which we accept God's dealings with us as good, and therefore without disputing or resisting."

Now, this is something you cannot learn from a book. You can only learn this when God deals with you directly. It means that as true disciples, when God deals with you about the issues of life, you do not rebel rather you see it as good and do not resist.

Please do not mistake what the Devil tries to throw at you, such as calamity, sickness, disease, poverty, or other bad and evil things, as God dealing with you about something concerning the issues of life. He will correct you in a godly way, but never through sickness, disease, or calamity.

Welcome the Dealings of God

When you are approaching God in your spiritual progression, and you become spiritually dependent on Him, the Holy Spirit may come to you and reveal areas where you are *not* dependent on Him. When He begins to quicken you in those areas, it is God dealing with you.

Jesus teaches that when God deals with you, you need to have a temper of spirit that receives correction—with mourning that works unto repentance. When you do not resist the dealings of God, such is meekness. By having a temper of spirit for correction, Jesus says that you will inherit and have possession of the earth.

Maybe you already know what it feels like when God is dealing with you about something. It is that little gnawing down in your spirit that prompts you to say, "You know, I've got to take care of that." That is the dealing of the Lord, but some people resist it.

"I know," they say. "I sense that, but He doesn't understand what I have going on." What? How can God not understand anything? That person is resisting what God is telling him or her.

More than likely, as with my congregation, you are well taught and you listen to the dealings of God. But, what a lot of Christians do not realize is that the pressures and problems they feel in their lives IS THEIR RESISTENCE to what God is dealing with them about; it is not necessarily the Devil's antics.

Meekness is accepting God's dealings as good, no matter what they are. It is accepting His direction gently, humbly, and with a soothing disposition.

When some people need to make a change, they are all grumpy and gripe about it. That is not meekness. In contrast, people who know they need to make a change and have a soothing disposition about it—that is meekness.

Meekness Takes Strength

As a true disciple, when you do not resist the dealings of God, but you choose to receive them with a gentle and smooth disposition, such composure and humility takes STRENGTH. It takes a strong person to be meek.

When I was in the Marines, the most intimidating, loud mouth, biggest guy never bothered me. You knew what he was all about because he kept telling you. The one you had to watch out for was the small, quiet, mild-mannered, meek one that would put a hurt on you before you could bat your eyes.

Yes, meek is to be mild and gentle, but it is also to be so strong and powerful that you can possess the earth.

"Blessed are the meek, for they shall inherit the earth."

How can the meek be so strong? Because of the blessing! But then, you yield that strength to the Lord.

Meekness is Yielded Strength

Another definition of meekness is *yielded strength*. Some people believe to be meek is to be wimpy. However, Moses is described as meek.

> *Now the man Moses was very meek, above all the men which were upon the face of the earth.*
>
> Numbers 12:3, KJV

Meekness does not translate to wimpy in any way.

I do not believe wimpy would be an accurate description of Moses. Before accepting a call into the ministry, Moses killed an Egyptian man with his own hands and buried him in the sand (Exod. 2:11-12). I would call that pretty strong. Of course, he had to repent. But, my point is that meekness does not translate to *wimpy* in any way—it is **yielded strength**.

However, most Christians' perception of being meek (and the world's for that matter) is that of an old, worn-out, sway-backed mare that can barely be ridden, when in actuality, being meek more closely resembles a thoroughbred horse in his prime—all muscled up and POWERFUL! Yet, all that strength is yielded to a little jockey on his back.

Now, I am not trying to compare God or the Holy Spirit to a little jockey. What I want is for you to see yourself like the thoroughbred—all muscled up in the power of meekness. You have strength, but you choose to gently, with a soothing disposition, yield it to the Lord. Meekness is yielded strength.

Meekness can also be defined as **power under authority**. Although the jockey is small, he has authority over the thoroughbred. The thoroughbred yields his power to him, just as we yield our power and strength to God.

What Meekness is NOT

Meekness is NOT weakness or being a coward. Many people think Christians are supposed to cower down in a corner and be weak. Such is not meekness.

Meekness is NOT passive acceptance of sin. It is not accepting sin and thinking it is okay. Meekness is being strong enough in a soothing, mild, and gentle disposition to stand against it. That is why the Church is being run over by social immorality; it will not take a stand because of a belief that meek means weak.

Meekness is NOT peace at any cost.

Meekness does NOT mean you never get angry. In fact, there is an anger that is godly. You can have an anger that you do not let the sun go down on because it needs to be dealt with, but the Word says to be angry and sin not (Eph. 4:26).

Biblical Definitions of Meekness

1. Humbly Receiving the Word of God.

Therefore lay aside all filthiness and overflow of wickedness, and receive with meekness the implanted word, which is able to save your souls.

James 1:21

Anytime you study your Bible and receive the Word with humility, you exhibit meekness. You are meek because you are humbly receiving the Word of God from me by reading this book.

2. Not Judging Harshly.

Brethren, if a man is overtaken in any trespass, you who are spiritual restore such a one in a spirit of gentleness, considering yourself lest you also be tempted.

Galatians 6:1

In other words, meekness does not judge someone harshly. Instead of judging harshly, we should attempt to restore that person.

3. Having a Helpful Attitude.

And a servant of the Lord must not quarrel but be gentle to all, able to teach, patient, in humility correcting those who are in opposition, if God perhaps will grant them repentance, so that they may know the truth.

II Timothy 2:24-25

Meekness is not being quarrelsome, but gentle to all men. It is to teach and instruct those who oppose you in hopes God will give them mercy. Meekness is a readiness to help others.

4. Keeping Unity and Peace.

I, therefore, the prisoner of the Lord, beseech you to walk worthy of the calling with which you were called, with all lowliness and gentleness ["meekness" KJV], with longsuffering, bearing with one another in love, endeavoring to keep the unity of the Spirit in the bond of peace.

Ephesians 4:1-3

Meekness is being gentle and patient—always striving to walk in love and harmony with those around you.

5. Clothed in Forgiveness.

Therefore, as the elect of God, holy and beloved, put on tender mercies, kindness, humility, meekness, longsuffering; bearing with one another, and forgiving one another, if anyone has a complaint against another; even as Christ forgave you, so you also must do.

Colossians 3:12-13

Meekness is being clothed in forgiveness. Have you ever known a person who just seems to forgive no matter what happens to them? I know people like that. Brother Kenneth Copeland is like that.

When I was his associate minister, I watched people attack him viciously. They still do. And he just walks in love.

One time in particular, I remember another preacher (a preacher with a big name) wrote an article about Bro. Copeland, just blasting him.

Now, I was with Bro. Copeland day and night. If he preached, I was breathing the air he breathed. I heard every word. I was there, and I knew the things this other man was saying just were not true.

Well, I am here to tell you, I was mad! I was not meek, and I was not forgiving. When I told Bro. Copeland about it, I said, "Let me show you this!"

He said, "I don't want to read it."

"But," I quickly added. "Don't you see what it says?"

He quickly replied, "I don't want to read it." Then he explained, "Billy, the two times you get into trouble is when others are either speaking good about you or speaking bad about you. If they are speaking good, you can get into pride, and if they speak bad, you get angry. So, I'd just rather not know."

He followed with, "Here is what I want you to do. Go down to the accounting department and get a check for five thousand dollars made out to this man's ministry (and this was a long time ago). Then, go buy him a gift to go with that, bring it to me, and I'll sign it—then send it to him in my name."

I am thinking, "Yeah, okay, I will, but I'm going to put some powder on it or something." Praise God, I did not sabotage it in any way, but my point is that Bro. Copeland operated in meekness.

He could have used his television program and all the resources he had to attack back, but instead he said this: "A gift in secret pacifies anger (Prov. 21:14). I forgive him already. He doesn't even know that I have, but I don't need him to know."

Meekness is being clothed in forgiveness.

There is something I have learned: If someone wrongs you, God will deal with you about forgiveness almost immediately. Why? Because He has forgiven us all at the cost of His son. Meekness is to walk in forgiveness.

The Blessings of the Meek

According to Jesus, there are blessings that come from being meek. The following are blessings you can expect:

1. Guidance in Judgment.

The meek will he guide in judgment . . .

Psalm 25:9, KJV

If you are meek, then God will guide you in judgment.

2. Knowledge of God's Way.

. . . the meek will he teach his way.

Psalm 25:9, KJV

The second part of this verse says that the meek will have knowledge of God's way. That is good news.

3. Satisfaction.

The meek shall eat and be satisfied.

Psalm 22:26, KJV

Another blessing of being meek is being satisfied. Now, this is what God says, not me. Therefore, if God wrote it, and we are talking about God writing through His Holy Spirit as He moved on men to write inspired of God, then it is true (II Pet. 1:21).

This Psalm says that to be meek is to be blessed by being satisfied. That is just a good deal! Have you ever eaten a meal, and then you were full and satisfied? That is the same feeling you will experience by being meek.

4. Inheritance of the Earth and Peace.

The meek shall inherit the earth; and shall delight themselves in the abundance of peace.

Psalm 37:11, KJV

Another blessing of being meek is inheritance of the earth, which means to occupy and possess, and the abundance of peace. In other words, you will not be affected by all the uneasiness, confusion, and strife going on in the world. You will have ownership of that which you set your hand to do, and you will have an abundance of peace.

People have spent untold millions on secular ways to find peace, but there are none. After accepting Jesus Christ as your Lord, there is an ABUNDANCE of peace that comes with being meek.

5. Receive Help from God.

The Lord lifteth up the meek: he casteth the wicked down to the ground.

Psalms 147:6, KJV

The Lord lifting up the meek means to receive help from God. But the wicked, He will cast down to the ground. A promise to receive help in life from God is an invaluable blessing!

6. Increased Joy.

The meek also shall increase their joy in the Lord, and the poor among men shall rejoice in the Holy One of Israel.

Isaiah 29:19, KJV

If you are meek, then you are joyful, and your joy will increase. If there were ever a time the Body of Christ needed joy, because the joy of the Lord is our strength (Neh. 8:10), it is right now. Isaiah says that you will have increased joy if you are meek.

You can tell your friends that you have the secret to joy and peace.

I am not saying that someone who does not appear to have joy is not meek, but one of the blessings of meekness is increased joy. Peace and joy are what a lot of people are looking for right now. You can tell your friends that you have the secret to joy and peace—it is meekness.

7. Instruct the Lost.

In meekness instructing those that oppose themselves; if God peradventure will give them repentance to the acknowledging of the truth.

II Timothy 2:25, KJV

The *New Living Translation* reads:

Gently instruct those who oppose the truth. Perhaps God will change those people's hearts, and they will learn the truth.

This verse says that if you are meek (gentle), you will be able to instruct the lost and those who oppose the truth. I believe most Christians at one time or another have asked God for the right words to say to those who oppose the truth. According to this Scripture, it is through meekness this ability comes. What a blessing that is!

To recap, we have just read seven specific blessings for those who are meek. If you walk in meekness, the Word says that you are:

1. Blessed with God's guidance in judgment;
2. Blessed with knowledge of God's way;
3. Blessed with satisfaction;
4. Blessed with inheritance of the earth and abundant peace;
5. Blessed with help from God;
6. Blessed with increased joy; and
7. Blessed with instructing the lost and those who oppose the truth.

Wow! What wonderful benefits from the Word of God concerning meekness. The reason I am providing so much

Scripture is because I do not want this important aspect of developing godly character to be swept away as a fancy little teaching about being meek. No, I want you to see what the Bible really has to say about meekness and its importance to true disciples.

The good news is that meekness is available to every one of us; however, it takes time to develop.

Developing Meekness

It took Moses forty years to develop meekness. From the time he fled Egypt after killing a man until the time he left the wilderness to lead the children of Israel out of Egypt took forty, long years. And the Word says he was the meekest of all men.

So, it takes time to develop meekness. I am not saying forty years is the standard, thank God! We can get it done more quickly. But, meekness does take time. You have to be patient.

Working Definition of Meekness

If we look at our spiritual progression to this point: Meekness is having a soothing disposition that causes a godly sorrow (as God deals with you) because you are spiritually dependent on Him. Through meekness, you receive the blessing of God's guidance, assistance, and knowledge of His ways. Meekness gives you an inheritance, satisfaction, joy, peace, and a gentleness to instruct the lost and those who oppose the truth.

Meekness has nothing to do with being weak. It has all to do with yielded strength to God, and it is with yielded strength that you develop a relationship with God that is worthy of a true disciple.

Meekness has nothing to do with being weak.

A true disciple with yielded strength is like a strong thoroughbred horse running and darting through varying conditions with agility and power, and all at the command and guidance of a still, small voice within. He yields his strength gladly as he navigates the issues of life with precision because of the blessing, and with a gentle spirit across the earth he possesses.

CHAPTER 8

BLESSED ARE THOSE WHO HUNGER AND THIRST FOR RIGHTEOUSNESS

Blessed are those who hunger and thirst for righteousness, for they shall be filled.

—Matthew 5:6

On our trek toward true discipleship, we have emptied ourselves before God and have become spiritually dependent (poor in spirit), we have sorrowed in a godly way for where we have fallen short and have repented (mourning), then, realizing who we are in Christ, we have yielded our strength to Him (meekness).

At the same time, as we meditate and turn over and over in our minds the Word and other aspects associated with these characteristics, such thoughts drop into our hearts and produce a flow of **godly character** to deal with the issues of life.

IT IS HERE WE ARRIVE AT THE THRONE OF GOD!

By being blessed, we have become spiritually prosperous and are empowered to progress through these first few characteristics of a true disciple. We have been privileged to have God deal with us on each level and be allowed to repent and move forward. All the while, the blessings flowing through us have allowed our issues of life to be greeted with happiness, success, and a godly character. Now we arrive at Matthew 5:6. Jesus says,

Blessed and fortunate and happy and spiritually prosperous (in that state in which the born-again

*child of God **enjoys His favor and salvation**) are those who hunger and thirst for righteousness (uprightness and right standing with God), for they shall be completely satisfied!* (AMP)

Notice, a disciple enjoys God's *favor* AND *salvation*—not just *salvation*. Not everyone who enjoys the *salvation* of God necessarily enjoys the *favor* of God. I do not know about you, but I want the favor of God on my life. In order to have this favor, you must hunger and thirst for righteousness.

God Says What He Means

Why do you think Jesus chooses the words *hunger* and *thirst*? He could say, "Blessed are you if you *desire* and *seek* after the righteousness of God."

When you study your Bible, you must realize that the Word says what God intends for it to say. That is why we must go to the Greek and Hebrew origin of words sometimes to denote their meanings. The choice of words used are directed by the Lord, and the words Jesus uses in this verse are what the Father intends for Him to say. Jesus says,

*"Blessed are those who **hunger and thirst** for righteousness, for they shall be filled."*

In the Greek, Jesus actually uses the words *hungry* and *thirsty* as in a continual need of fulfillment; you are blessed if you are hungry and thirsty for righteousness, constantly. Hunger and thirst are natural appetites.

Jesus chooses these words because they can never be *completely* satisfied, but they are *continually* satisfied. You do not get hungry, eat once, and then never have the need to eat again. It does not work that way. You have an appetite that needs to be fed continually.

The same goes for drinking water. You do not thirst once, have a drink, and then never thirst again. No, we all have natural appetites called *hunger* and *thirst* that need to be satisfied continually.

Jesus says, "Blessed [enjoying enviable favor] are you in dealing with the issues of life when you are poor in spirit, mournful, meek, and hungry and thirsty for continual satisfaction of God's ways."

In other words, you do not go into the presence of God and then back out again. You hunger and thirst for His continual presence. You want to stay there every day. You are hungry in a continual way.

Hunger for Righteousness

The word *hunger* in the Greek is *peinao*, which means "a craving and urgent need for food." Jesus is saying that we must constantly, with urgency, crave and hunger for the righteousness of God—always hungering for more. Although He will fill you, there will always be more for which to hunger.

Another definition for *hunger* is "an uneasy sensation occasioned by a lack of food." That is what your body experiences naturally when in need of food. Every one of us has been hungry before, and every one of us has been full. Some have been more full than others (I am talking about myself!), but we have all had that occasional sensation and craving for food.

Jesus says that you will stay blessed if you continue to crave spiritual food that can only come from the Word and God's presence. And if you do not have spiritual food—the Word—there should be an uneasy sensation in you that hungers for the spiritual fullness the Word gives. It is a continual craving and a hunger down in your spirit and soul for the things of God.

> *You will stay blessed if you continue to crave spiritual food.*

In fact, if you ever get to the place where you think you know the Word and have arrived, then you have just stopped hungering and thirsting for righteousness. You should not be able to go very long without an uneasy feeling down in your spirit that you need the Word—the bread of life.

Thirst for Righteousness

The word *thirst* in the Greek is *dipsao*, which means "a desire for liquids," and "a dryness in the mouth and throat that causes a craving for liquid." Jesus says that you will walk blessed through the issues of life you face if your character is sustained by thirsting for the things of God. You will crave the washing of the water of the Word on a continual, regular basis in the same manner a dry mouth craves water.

What is Righteousness?

"Blessed are those who hunger and thirst for **righteousness***, for they shall be filled."*

What is the meaning of the word *righteousness* in this verse? If you go to the Greek, Jesus uses the word *dikaiosune*, which means "the character or quality of being right or just." *Young's Analytical Concordance* simply translates it as "rightness."

According to *Vine's*, the word *rightwiseness* more clearly expresses the meaning of *dikaiosune*, which denotes an attribute of God. The word *righteousness* does not come from the Hebrew or Greek, but is an old English word meaning "to right a ship."

If you consider the word *rightwiseness* and its meaning, you could say, "Blessed are those who hunger, crave, desire, and have a constant appetite for the things of God and for His revealed will. As you hunger and thirst for God's 'wiseness' in your life, you will be filled."

It did not take long after I was saved to realize that God is not only a whole lot smarter than me, but he is a whole lot wiser than I will *ever* be.

Righteousness is an attribute of God, and not just a way of doing things; it is a characteristic.

Jesus says that when you hunger and thirst for this characteristic of God in the same way you would seek food when you are hungry, or seek water on a hot day, then you will be filled! The actual word *filled* in the Greek is *chortazo*, which means "to feed" or "to fill or satisfy with food."

"Blessed are those who hunger and thirst for righteousness, for they shall be filled."

Jesus Answers the Prophets of Old

Interestingly, Jesus addressing a need to hunger and thirst for righteousness is Him answering a call and cry of many Old Testament prophets, particularly the psalmist David.

As the deer pants for the water brooks, so pants my soul for You, O God. My soul thirsts for God, for the living God. When shall I come and appear before God?

Psalm 42:1-2

Do you hear the cry there? David is thirsting, panting, and seeking God as a deer for water.

Today's English Version states:

As a deer longs for a stream of cool water, so I long for you, O God. I thirst for you, the living God. When can I go and worship in your presence?

David is saying, "When can I quench my thirst? I am longing for your presence."

Thirsting for God is contagious. If I take a sip of water while I am preaching, often I can see others in my congregation look at me as though they wish they had a sip. Why? Because thirst touches your natural appetite. It is the same when thirsting for God. Thirsting for God is contagious.

While in the wilderness of Judah, David writes this Psalm:

O God, You are my God; early will I seek You; my soul thirsts for You; my flesh longs for You in a dry and thirsty land where there is no water.

So I have looked for You in the sanctuary, to see your power and your glory. Because Your lovingkindness is better than life, my lips shall praise You. Thus I will bless You while I live; I will lift up my hands in Your name.

My soul shall be satisfied as with marrow and fatness, and my mouth shall praise you with joyful lips.

When I remember You on my bed, I meditate on You in the night watches, because you have been my help, therefore in the shadow of Your wings I will rejoice.

My soul follows close behind You; Your right hand upholds me.

Psalm 63:1-8

David goes on to say that not only will God uphold him, but He will fight against his enemies. Therefore, when you will hunger and thirst after God, He will even take care of your enemies, including those who will persecute you for righteousness' sake and Jesus' sake.

But notice, David is saying, "I am hungering and thirsting for God. I am thirsting for that filling." He indicates that this feeling is not something he is only going to experience once; it is something he must keep doing.

David says, "WHEN? When will it be? God, I'm thirsty. WHEN will I be filled?"

Jesus Answers David's Cry

David's earnest questions are answered by Jesus in Matthew 5:6. It is part of the good news! Jesus sits His disciples down and tells them that they will no longer have to cry and ask when their hunger and thirst for God will be quenched. The time is NOW!

Jesus says, "Blessed are you when you hunger and thirst because **YOU WILL BE FILLED!**" How? By continuing to hunger and thirst after God! For as you hunger and thirst for the rightwiseness of God, which is God's way of thinking and doing, YOU WILL BE SATISFIED.

What you hunger and thirst for reveals the condition of your heart.

Guard Your Hunger and Thirst

There is something to consider as you hunger and thirst. Give yourself a serious examination now and then as to the object of your hunger and thirst. Why? Because what you hunger and thirst for reveals the condition of your heart. Make sure it is the progression we have discussed through which your hunger and thirst derives. Otherwise, you can get off track quickly.

Some may not believe that to be so. They say, "Well, God knows my heart. He'll get me to where I need to go." Oh, no, no. You must guard your heart because whatever you hunger and thirst for **will fill you**—good or bad.

In Romans, Paul writes concerning filling the appetites of the flesh:

> *For such persons do not serve our Lord Christ but their own appetites and base desires.*

> Romans 16:18, AMP

Cravings and appetites of the flesh will affect your hunger and thirst for God. What you hunger and thirst for reveals what is in your heart.

> *Those who live according to the flesh set their minds on the things of the flesh, but those who live according to the Spirit, the things of the Spirit.*

> Romans 8:5

Remember what we have learned, that which you think about consistently will eventually get into your heart. As you think, so are you. Who you are enters through your thought life. Paul describes those who ponder, or *set their minds* to the flesh as living according to their flesh. Living according to your fleshly appetites will cause you to desire things of the flesh.

When I was Associate Minister for Kenneth Copeland Ministries, Gloria Copeland was just starting her teaching ministry. I will never forget something she taught. She said, "What you give your attention to governs your desires." When she said that, it was written on the tablets of my heart: What I give my attention to controls my desires.

Interestingly, it does not work the opposite way. You might think you desire something first and then give it your attention. No, recall what Paul says, *"Those who live according to the flesh **set their minds** on the things of the flesh."* **It is what you give your attention to that you will desire.**

For example, if you do not care for football and do not give it your attention, you are not going to race home after church to see a ballgame. But, if you do give football your attention, you will desire it. The same thing is true with hungering and thirsting.

Further, the appetites of your heart *control your condition.* If you are giving most of your attention to your favorite team and that is where your hunger and desire is, then that is what is controlling how you deal with the issues of life.

If this is the case, why go to God with your needs? Why not go to your favorite team? Such is the object of your hunger and thirst, right? Sounds silly to a Christian, but trust me, the attentions of your heart will control you. And, worse still, hungering and thirsting for things other than God will bring a halt to your development as a true disciple.

> *Those who are living the life of the flesh [catering to the appetites and impulses of their carnal nature] cannot please or satisfy God, or be acceptable to Him.*
>
> Romans 8:8, AMP

Therefore, in order to be blessed according to our subject text, Matthew 5:6, you need to keep your appetites and attention on God.

As a way of illustration, sometimes during the course of the day we can get hungry between meals, and there is a temptation to snack. Now, snacking is not necessarily sinning; however, eating snacks between meals will dampen your appetite for the next meal, in the natural. Likewise, when your attention is "snacking" on things of the flesh, your hunger and thirst for God's righteousness will be dampened. Conversely, the more your appetite is satisfied with God's righteousness, His right thinking and way of doing things, the more dissatisfied you will become with the ways of the world.

What controls your hunger controls the issues of your life.

What controls your hunger controls the issues of your life. Wow! Think about it. What you put your attention to is what controls the issues of your life.

What Controls Your Hunger?

What about you? What controls your hunger and how you respond to the issues before you?

Let me test your spiritual appetite:

1. Do you see through your own false righteousness? I am not talking about whether or not someone else knows when you are faking it. But, if you can see through yourself, then change can come.

2. Do you realize how much you need Jesus and how helpless you are without him?

3. Do you avoid everything that is opposed to righteousness? Not bits and pieces, but everything?

4. Are your priorities in order?

5. Do you always put yourself in a position to be filled? Remember, where you position yourself controls your appetite and controls your filling. If you want to be filled with the glory of God and the power of God, then you should position yourself for such to take place.

6. What is the issue flowing out of your heart? Is your driving force an overwhelming desire to know God and to be like Him?

If your answer to these questions is yes, then you will be filled and satisfied. Jesus promises this.

Hunger and Thirst for God
Creates an Intimate Relationship

Recall the account of Moses and the children of Israel. After all of the miracles and life experiences Moses faced up to and through his dealing with Pharaoh, God finally led the children of Israel out of Egypt (Exod. 12:51). Then from Exodus chapters 13 through 33, which is twenty chapters of history and spiritual growth, the Word says,

> *So the Lord spoke to Moses face to face, as a man speaks to his friend.*

> Exodus 33:11

God was able to share with Moses in a way that can only be established through growth and maturity, and it takes time. It comes by growing in the things God wants you to grow in. It is a spiritual progression.

As you move in your progression toward God, you establish an intimate, personal, face-to-face relationship with Him. The character you develop as you deal with the issues of life comes from a lifestyle of hungering and thirsting for the ways of God.

What Have We Learned?

As a true disciple, you walk through life spiritually dependent on God (poor in spirit), you have a godly sorrow for the things in which you have fallen short (mourning). This leads you to repentance. Then, you yield your strength and power to His authority (meekness). This causes you to hunger and thirst after righteousness, and God fills and satisfies you.

BUT, YOU DO NOT STOP THERE.

Outpouring to Others

Next, you take that filling and allow it to overflow to others. The result is the merciful, the pure in heart, and the peacemakers. Such is Jesus' subject of Matthew 5:7-9 that we will examine in the Chapters to follow.

Those characteristics are not attained through a progression toward God, but *after* a progression toward God. You do not need to make peace between you and God because Jesus has already done that. It is talking about true disciples toward mankind. You go out into the world with your filling.

Of course, you cannot be merciful unless you spend time around He who is mercy. And, you are not going to get to this place once and for all. Such is the result of a spiritual progression that you do over and over again. You are filled and will continue to be filled.

CHAPTER 9

BLESSED ARE THE MERCIFUL

Blessed are the merciful,
for they shall obtain mercy.

—*Matthew 5:7*

Up to now, we have examined the spiritual progression of a true disciple toward God. At its end, we have established an intimate relationship with our Lord through hungering and thirsting for His righteousness. There we have been filled and satisfied, and by staying in His presence, continue to be filled. Now it is time to take that godly filling to the world. The first step in this spiritual progression is being **merciful**. Jesus says,

"Blessed are the merciful [you and me—His true disciples], *for they* [true disciples] *shall obtain mercy."*

The *New Living Translation* says,

"God blesses those who are merciful, for they will be shown mercy."

The Message uses this commentary:

"You're blessed when you care. At the moment of being 'care-full,' you find yourselves cared for."

In other words, when you are merciful, you will be "mercied" or cared for yourself.

The Greek word for *merciful* is *eleemon,* which means "not simply possessed of pity, but actively compassionate."

Being merciful is not just *feeling sorry* for the poor; it is being blessed to where you are able to *meet the needs* of the poor. It is having a godly compassion. In fact, *eleemon* also means "those who are like God." We are to be merciful in the same fashion that God is merciful.

Being merciful is taking the need of a person and having adequate provisions to meet that need. That is why people who preach poverty are actually cursing themselves because when you preach poverty and put people in that mindset, you remove that person from being adequately able to be merciful toward others. Why? Because they do not have adequate provisions to help others.

> *Our working definition of merciful is LOVE IN ACTION.*

Being merciful is kindness that manifests to those in need, and a readiness to help. It is a desire to relieve the suffering of others. Such is God's desire for all of us, and it is how true disciples present themselves to the world.

Our working definition of merciful is LOVE IN ACTION.

Jesus says, "Blessed are those who have the God kind of love springing into action, for this is the same *love in action* that will come back to them."

To further understand being merciful, let us look at two different aspects of God: God's grace and God's mercy. They are not the same. God is gracious, and God is merciful. They both come from God, and they are both good, but how are they different?

God's Grace

Now, this is just a country boy's definition, but *grace* is God giving us what we *do not* deserve. You cannot earn it, and you do not deserve it. That is grace. None of us deserve the grace of God; however, in His love, God allows grace to flow through the Lord Jesus Christ.

God's Mercy

On the other hand, *mercy* is God *not* giving us what we *do* deserve. That is mercy! And when God blesses us and has mercy on us—boy, that is grace.

How are God's grace and mercy different? GRACE is when God gives us things that we do not deserve, but MERCY is when God, as love in action, does not give us what we DO deserve, which is punishment. What we deserve is judgment and hell, BUT, God had MERCY and gave us Jesus who brought GRACE. Hallelujah!

How to be Merciful

In order to understand further how to develop the merciful aspects of a disciple's character, we need to comprehend God's capacity for mercy.

God's Side of Mercy

1. God is Merciful.

First of all, God IS merciful. Such is His character. Moreover, His mercy and kindness is everlasting.

Through the Lord's mercies we are not consumed, because His compassions fail not. They are new every morning; great is Your faithfulness.

Lamentations 3:22-23

2. God's Mercy is Unfailing.

We must understand that God's mercy goes far beyond our ability to be merciful. Why? Although God's compassions do not fail, our emotions tend to fluctuate. We might be merciful one day, but then the next day watch mercy fly out the window because of this or that happening in our lives.

Our ability to be merciful does not reach the degree of God's mercy. HOWEVER, when filled in His presence, we can take a portion of His mercy to the world. God expects us to be merciful by demonstrating love in action so that we may walk in the character of the blessed. Yet, God's mercy goes beyond our abilities.

3. God's Mercy for Salvation.

It is by God's mercy we are saved.

Not by works of righteousness which we have done, but according to His mercy He saved us, through the washing of regeneration and renewing of the Holy Spirit.

Titus 3:5

All of us who are born again were saved ONLY because God was merciful. If not, He would have given us what we deserved: JUDGMENT!

That knowledge alone is enough for me to get up each morning and shout and holler, "Thank God, through His mercy He saved us!" You and I do not have that ability. God demonstrates this mercy through the Lord Jesus Christ.

4. God's Mercy is Full.

I am going to give you another country boy's definition, which is God's mercy is not *short-fused*. In case you have not heard the term "short-fused," it means just as it sounds: The fuse to someone's anger bomb is very short—it does not take much to cause an explosion. Conversely, God is not quick to anger. His mercy is full, not short-fused.

The Lord is gracious and full of compassion, slow to anger and great in mercy. The Lord is good to all, and His tender mercies are over all His works!

Psalm 145:8-9

This verse does not mean that God never gets angry. There is an anger that is not sin (Eph. 4:26). The good news for us is that God's mercy is FULL, and not short-fused.

For example, when God is showing me something in the Word, I know He probably wants to get it over to me quickly, but I like to see it in about eight different places. I am sure if it were not for God's mercy, He might say, "Just hush up, and do what I tell you." But, He does not. God is patient, and not short-fused.

5. God's Mercy is Rich.

Finally, we see that God is rich in mercy.

But God, who is rich in mercy, because of His great love with which He loved us, even when we were dead in trespasses, made us alive together with Christ (by grace you have been saved).

Ephesians 2:4-5

If God is rich in mercy, then it is a rich, rich. God is rich! Rich in this passage means wealthy abundance. And, everything He has, He desires for us all to walk in those same blessings. Such is why these are the characteristics of the **blessed**.

Now that we have seen God's side of mercy, let us look at a disciple's side of mercy.

A Disciple's Side of Mercy

Jesus says that His disciples are to be merciful. Our definition of merciful is "love in action" in the same manner that God is merciful. The only way we can obtain that selfless level of mercy in our character is by the spiritual progression up to this point.

We have been in the presence of God because of hungering and thirsting for righteousness. God has been faithful and has filled us. Now we have turned that filling to mankind, and the first characteristic that will reveal itself is being merciful.

Luke 6:27-38 is probably one of the most incorrectly taught parables in the Bible.

As we have discovered, it is not just enough to have pity, we must have *love in action* to meet the needs of others.

In Luke 6:27-38, Jesus delivers a parable addressing a disciple's side of mercy. It is the parable that speaks of "turning the other cheek," and it is probably one of the most incorrectly taught parables in the Bible.

The subjects often taught from this parable are (1) love your enemies, (2) do not judge, and (3) prosperity. Although there is truth in all of these subjects, I believe there is a more powerful underlying message Jesus is trying to teach His disciples, which is mercy.

Watch the flow, and you will see what I am talking about. Jesus is using this parable to demonstrate ways in which a disciple can show mercy.

*"But I say to you who hear: Love your enemies, **do good** to those who hate you, bless those who curse you, and pray for those who spitefully use you.*

"To him who strikes you on the one cheek, offer the other also. And from him who takes away your cloak, do not withhold your tunic either.

"Give to everyone who asks of you. And from him who takes away your goods do not ask them back.

"And just as you want men to do to you, you also do to them likewise.

"But if you love those who love you, what credit is that to you? For even sinners love those who love them.

*"And if you **do good** to those who **do good** to you, what credit is that to you? For even sinners do the same.*

"And if you lend to those from whom you hope to receive back, what credit is that to you? For even sinners lend to sinners to receive as much back.

*"But love your enemies, **do good**, and lend, hoping for nothing in return; and your reward will be great, and you will be sons of the Most High. For He is kind to the unthankful and evil.*

*"Therefore be **merciful**, just as your Father also is merciful.*

"Judge not, and you shall not be judged. Condemn not, and you shall not be condemned. Forgive, and you will be forgiven.

"Give, and it will be given to you: good measure, pressed down, shaken together, and running over will be put into your bosom. For with the same measure that you use, it will be measured back to you."

Luke 6:27-38

Notice the running theme of striving to "do good." Jesus mentions nothing else four times except to do good. Then, He sums up the theme of *doing good* into a characteristic of being **merciful**.

*"Therefore be **merciful**, just as your Father also is merciful."*

Jesus teaches that a disciple can show mercy by doing good. **The first subject of this parable is to "do good."** The subject IS NOT allowing someone to beat you on the face two or three times, slap you around, and take everything you have. No, Jesus is delivering a parable, and the first subject of the parable is to "do good."

The second subject is to be "merciful." After Jesus says to do good four times, then He says, "Therefore, because you are DOING GOOD, be MERCIFUL just as your father is also merciful."

Again, the subject of this parable is not allowing someone to strike you on the left side, then you, like a dummy, get up and turn the other cheek for him to strike you again. Nor is it about someone asking you for your last dime, and then you give it to them and not pay your bills.

The point Jesus is making is to be merciful. He is showing His disciples the degree of mercy that is expected from them.

*"Therefore be **merciful**, just as your Father also is merciful. Judge not, and you shall not be judged. Condemn not, and you shall not be condemned. Forgive, and you will be forgiven."*

Continuing with verse 38:

"Give, and it will be given to you: good measure, pressed down, shaken together, and running over will be put into your bosom. For with the same measure that you use, it will be measured back to you."

When you take this parable in its entirety, the subject of this verse is not the giving of finances and expecting a return, although it has a double reference meaning and is an absolute truth. The subject of the parable is **doing good and being merciful—even to your enemies!** Doing good to your enemies means giving them what they need, whether it be possessions, money, food, clothes, prayer, or whatever is needed—LOVE IN ACTION!

One of the reasons our nation has lasted these last fifty years, in spite of a bunch of yahoos who have tried to take God out of everything, is because our nation has remained merciful. We give money, even to our enemies.

The entire subject matter of Luke chapter 6 is the mercy expected from a disciple, and mercy is love in action. Our part of being merciful is to do good, even to our enemies. Be merciful.

Let us go back now to Luke 6:29 and look at that verse a little more closely.

"To him who strikes you on the one cheek, offer the other also. And from him who takes away your cloak, do not withhold your tunic either."

If you just glaze over this verse with a religious mind, you will miss the point being made. The subject of this parable is showing mercy by doing good, and now verse 29 tells us that another way to show mercy is to forgive.

The third subject of this parable is walking in forgiveness. The reason you can turn the other cheek is because you have forgiven. To be merciful, you have to forgive. You cannot be merciful if you have unforgiveness toward someone. You cannot. Such is the point Jesus is making here.

Further, your motivation for turning the other cheek, or forgiving, matters as well. If you find yourself thinking, "We'll, I'm going to forgive you because God says I have to, but I don't want to," then that is not love in action, but sacrifice. Sacrifice is not the same as mercy.

To be merciful, you must walk in forgiveness.

Mercy, Not Sacrifice

To be merciful, you must walk in forgiveness. Forgiveness is based on God's mercy in spite of what has been done.

> *For I desired mercy, and not sacrifice; and the knowledge of God more than burnt offerings.*
>
> Hosea 6:6, KJV

What does this mean? Sacrifice means that you forgive and love others because you HAVE to. Mercy says, "I forgive you, just because I've been forgiven. I love you because that is my character."

Jesus says, *"I desire mercy and not sacrifice."* He wants His disciples to do good out of mercy, and not because a pastor or teacher told them to do so. It is done because it is a disciple's character to be merciful. A true disciple says, "I love because He first loved me. I forgive you, because He first forgave me. I show compassion, love in action, because He sent His Son to die for me, which is love in action."

117

In the Gospel of Matthew, Jesus quotes Hosea 6:6 in response to being questioned by the Pharisees when His disciples pick grain to eat on the Sabbath.

At that time Jesus went through the grainfields on the Sabbath. And His disciples were hungry, and began to pluck heads of grain and to eat. And when the Pharisees saw it, they said to Him, "Look, Your disciples are doing what is not lawful to do on the Sabbath!"

But He said to them, "Have you not read what David did when he was hungry, he and those who were with him: how he entered the house of God and ate the showbread which was not lawful for him to eat, nor for those who were with him, but only for the priests?

"Or have you not read in the law that on the Sabbath the priests in the temple profane the Sabbath, and are blameless? Yet I say to you that in this place there is One greater than the temple.

"But if you had known what this means, 'I desire mercy and not sacrifice,' you would not have condemned the guiltless. For the Son of Man is Lord even of the Sabbath."

Matthew 12:1-8

The *New Living Translation* interprets verse 7 this way:

But you would not have condemned my innocent disciples if you knew the meaning of this Scripture: 'I want you to show mercy, not offer sacrifices.'

The *Amplified Bible* says this:

*And if you had only known what this saying means, **I desire mercy [readiness to help, to spare, to forgive]** rather than sacrifice and sacrificial victims, you would not have condemned the guiltless.*

Now, go back to verse 2. There is something about mercy and the Lord I want you to see.

And when the Pharisees saw it, they said to Him, "Look, Your disciples are doing what is not lawful to do on the Sabbath!"

Other translations in the Greek bear out that the Pharisees were angry. The *New Living Translation* says they "protested."

In other words, the Pharisees are not simply questioning Jesus about the unlawfulness of picking grain on the Sabbath. No, they are angry and protesting. They are saying, "How dare you let them do something unlawful; you need to punish them."

Jesus says, "If you knew that I would desire that you show mercy, not sacrifice, you would understand. More than your offering of sacrifices, I would have you spare, forgive, and have a readiness to help."

What the Pharisees want is for Jesus to retaliate and punish His disciples. *Now, this is the point I want you to catch.*

You cannot be merciful to someone you do not have the power to retaliate against.

Jesus has the power. Because of the law, He could discipline His disciples, judge them, and retaliate against them. However, He shows them mercy.

You cannot mercy someone unless you have the ability NOT to mercy them. You cannot show mercy unless you have the ability to show the reverse. Being merciful is when you COULD judge it differently, and you have the ability, power, and right to judge it differently, but you are merciful.

Mercy is Refraining from Retaliation

God could have wiped us all out. He could have made every one of us crispy critters and just changed this whole deal because He has the power. Because He COULD retaliate against the sin, He was in a position to be merciful. You can only be merciful when you have the ability to retaliate. Therefore, when someone does something, and you have the ability to retaliate, Jesus says in Luke chapter 6 and Matthew chapter 12, you can choose to be merciful.

You cannot walk in unforgiveness unless you have the ability to forgive. In fact, you do not qualify to walk in unforgiveness against someone unless they trespass against you. Further, if you have the opportunity to forgive and you do not, it weakens your character, and you will not walk in the blessing of being shown mercy yourself. I choose to be merciful. I must forgive those who trespass against me.

Beloved, do not avenge yourselves, but rather give place to wrath; for it is written, "Vengeance is Mine, I will repay," says the Lord.

Therefore "If your enemy is hungry, feed him; if he is thirsty, give him a drink; for in so doing you will heap coals of fire on his head."

Do not be overcome by evil, but overcome evil with good.

Romans 12:19-21

In this passage, the theme of showing mercy by doing good to your enemies, by demonstrating love in action, is reinforced. And according to our subject text in Matthew 5:7, Jesus says that by being merciful, you will obtain mercy. However, you do not obtain God's mercy because you earn it by showing mercy to another. No, you obtain mercy because you sow it. What?

You do not obtain mercy from God because you earn it, but you obtain mercy from God because you sow it. Sow what? MERCY!

"While the earth remaineth, seedtime and harvest."

Genesis 8:22, KJV

What Paul is saying here, based on the teachings of Jesus, is not to worry about vengeance or retaliation. Instead, sow mercy. Then, you will be shown mercy, and there is a judgment day coming for the rest. God will judge it. **Mercy and justice flow from God.**

Jesus says, "You are blessed [happy, enjoying enviable favor, and spiritual prosperity] when you are merciful [love in action], for you shall be shown mercy [because mercy was sown]."

I do not know about you, but I am getting very excited about the blessings of a true disciple!

CHAPTER 10

BLESSED ARE THE PURE IN HEART

*B*LESSED ARE THE PURE IN HEART,
FOR THEY SHALL SEE GOD.

—MATTHEW 5:8

Consider the time period in which Jesus originally spoke these words. At that time, this would have been a very unusual statement to make. The new covenant had not yet been instituted; Jesus had not yet died on the cross or been raised from the dead, and the Holy Spirit had not yet been given.

Jesus is speaking to His disciples who are still under the Law: *"Blessed are the pure in heart, **for they shall see God.***" What? See God?

These original disciples were living in a time when the names of God were considered so holy that they could not be *mentioned*, let alone *see* God!

I am sure they believed their Father Abraham and Moses were able to see God, but Jesus tells them that THEY can see God. How? By being **pure in heart**. How does one become pure in heart?

> *Being compassionate and merciful leads to purity.*

After you are filled and satisfied in the presence of the Lord, you begin your spiritual progression toward man. Here, God uses you to minister to others with *compassion*; you become **merciful**.

When God uses you to help others in need, and you are demonstrating love in action, it causes you to want to live a life of purity before the Lord. It is through being compassionate and merciful that leads to purity and the desire to minister to others, which is being **pure in heart**. Jesus demonstrates purity of heart:

> *"But when He saw the multitudes, He was moved with compassion for them, because they were weary and scattered, like sheep with no shepherd."*

Matthew 9:36

What Purity Means

1. Not Tainted.

Have you noticed that the color *white* is often associated with purity? Did you know that *white* is not really a color, but an *absence* of color? In fact, if you take everything out of a picture that would color it, you would be left with white. That is probably the best definition you can give of *purity*—the absence of anything to taint it.

2. Cleansed.

If you search Noah Webster's original dictionary of 1828, which was written as a Christian dictionary to define Bible words *(American Dictionary of the English Language)*, you will find *purity* defined as "cleansed from filth and impurities."

The word *pure* in the Greek is *katharos*, which means "pure, as being cleansed."

Based on these definitions, being pure in heart is not so much something you have, but something from which you have been cleansed. It is the act of cleansing yourself of filth and impurities. For instance, have you ever worked outside, become all dirty and sweaty, and then someone you know approaches you? Almost the first thing you will say is "Don't come too close. I am all dirty, and I probably stink."

Afterwards, you will want to take a shower and get clean. It will make you feel better, look better, and smell better. Trust me, the people sitting around you are grateful. You cleansed yourself, but it did not change anything about the inside of you. You can be clean on the outside and still be the meanest sucker on the planet.

What Jesus is saying is "Blessed are those who remove impurities and filth of the heart." To be "pure" means to be cleansed from filth and impurities, and to be free from the defilement of sin.

3. Unmixed.

Noah Webster also defines *pure* as "unmixed with other matter." For instance, consider gold and silver. Separately, they are worth a great deal, but when they are mixed they are not as valuable. They are alloyed. Unalloyed means they are pure.

Sometimes conditions of the heart need to be unmixed and cleansed. Some of these conditions may not even be bad; yet, they may hinder you from hungering and thirsting for

God, from being spiritually dependent on God, or from being merciful and compassionate. Being pure in heart becomes a process of unmixing and cleansing of the heart.

4. Without Hypocrisy.

To be *pure* also means "to be free of guilt" and "without hypocrisy." To be pure in heart does not mean that you are the most holy thing on the face of the earth, but it does mean you live without *hypocrisy*.

The word *hypocrisy*, according to Noah Webster, means "a deceitful show of a good character." In the Greek, the word *hypocrite* means "stage actor" or "play acting." Jesus says,

> *Woe unto you, scribes and Pharisees, hypocrites! for ye devour widows' houses, and for a pretence make long prayer: therefore ye shall receive the greater damnation.*
>
> Matthew 23:14, KJV

Spiritually, purity is faith without pretense or a mask; it is faith without reading dialogue as an actor reads a script. I know preachers who are not even saved and read the Bible like a script. However, that is not faith in what the Word is saying; it is play acting.

I live in California, and I see this often. Take Hollywood, for example. Our society idolizes people who memorize dialogue from a script. The actors are probably nothing like the characters they play, yet people idolize them. In turn, studios pay them millions of dollars for *play acting.*

Pure in heart is to have faith without putting on an act.

Jesus is telling us that He wants us to be pure in heart, not play acting or reading from a script. He wants the real you. No mask.

It took Jesus being crucified to reconcile God with man; evidenced by the temple veil being torn in two (Matt. 27:51), and the veil being lifted from the hearts of those who turn to the Lord (II Cor. 3:15-16). Jesus is saying that in order to see God, you cannot do so through pretense, an actor's mask, or a veil. Pure in heart is to have faith without putting on an act.

5. Singleness of Purpose.

A final definition of *purity* is "singleness of purpose" or "being single-minded." It is to have a single, godly purpose in your heart.

Many more disciples could be pure in heart if they were not double and triple minded because *purity*, in its Greek form, is singleness of purpose.

As you live the character of the blessed, you will find that it does not stretch you many different ways. In fact, Jesus says that one of the character traits of a true disciple is becoming single in the purpose of your heart. You do not get sidetracked, mixed or alloyed, or infiltrated by many different things—you become one. As white is the absence of color, purity is singleness of purpose without outside influences or distractions.

Becoming Pure in Heart

As a true disciple, you must be unmixed, wear no mask, and be single in purpose in your heart for the Lord. This takes time. You do not get there instantly—it is a process.

If you are pure in heart, your character has progressed as Jesus said it would, and it is genuine. You possess a godly character, which is the opposite of being a hypocrite. You might say that when you are pure in heart, you have a genuine, godly character. And that is what we are striving for. That is what *The Character of the Blessed* is all about!

Definition of "Heart"

What about the word *heart*? Jesus says, *"pure in **heart**."*

"Blessed are the pure in heart, for they shall see God."

Jesus could have said, "pure in actions" or "pure in your thought life and how you treat people." However, He says, "Blessed is the character of those who are PURE in HEART."

Let us examine the meanings of the word *heart* more closely.

1. The Middle.

The word *heart* in our subject verse comes from the Greek word *kardia*. It is where we get the word *cardio* and *cardiac*. It means "the thoughts or feelings of the spirit and mind." Literal Greek means "the middle of something," such as the heart of the artichoke. It is called the heart because it is the middle.

Jesus says, "Blessed are those who are single in their purpose, unmasked, not play acting, not reading a script, and not pretending in any way. They are pure in their innermost heart."

2. Where God Dwells.

Vine's defines the *heart* as the "sphere of Divine influence." This is your spirit man, and it is where the Holy Spirit dwells if you are born again.

3. Location of Man's Mental and Moral Activity.

Vine's says the word *heart* represents "man's entire mental and moral activity." We can add this to our understanding of what Jesus is saying to His disciples: "Blessed are those who are pure, single in their purpose, unmixed, unalloyed, without filth, and who cleanse themselves of any impurities in their moral and mental activity."

Vine's definition goes on to include "both the rational and emotional elements" of man's mental and moral activity. In order to be blessed and see God, we must have a purity of the rational and emotional elements of our lives. Purity of heart means that, not only is your mental and moral activity pure, but the emotional and rational elements of your life are pure, as well.

What does that mean?

Well, when was the last time you rationally investigated, searched and looked inwardly at the elements in your own self rather than someone else? When was the last time you checked your emotions to make sure they were pure? In other words, what is going on in the "hidden springs" of your heart?

4. Hidden Springs.

The word *heart* represents the *hidden springs* of one's personal life. Remember our foundational Scripture in Proverbs 4:23?

*"Keep your heart with all diligence, for out of it spring **the issues of life**."*

What *Vine's* definition is revealing is that one's entire moral and mental activity flows from the hidden springs of one's personal life—their heart. This is the source from where your issues of life flow.

When you look at someone from the outside, all you see is their physical body or their flesh suit; however, that is not the real man. How do we know? Because as a man thinks **in**

his heart, so is he (Prov. 23:7). The real man is who he is in his heart. Of course, this includes women. When we refer to "man" it is the collective being of man or mankind.

So, what am I saying? The heart **contains** the real YOU, but it also **conceals** the real you. You might say, "Why would God place the real me in my heart, but then conceal the real me?" Because that is where He lives! You are abiding under the shadow of the Almighty, and such are the hidden things of God. You, by your character, determine what the "real you" reveals.

Have you ever had someone do something ugly to you, or say ugly things, but then say, "Well, that's not the real me." WRONG!

What does Jesus tell us in Matthew 12:34?

"Brood of vipers! How can you, being evil, speak good things? For out of the abundance of the heart the mouth speaks."

> *The real you is revealed when pressure comes.*

Actually, what you really saw WAS the **real them**. Instead of saying, "That's not the real me," they should have said, "That's not how I want to be."

The real you is not revealed when everything is going your way. That just reveals the "laid back" you. The real you is revealed when pressure comes.

Rather let it be the hidden person of the heart, with the incorruptible beauty of a gentle and quiet spirit, which is very precious in the sight of God.

I Peter 3:4

The "hidden person" of the heart is the real person. The *King James Version* says, *"hidden man"* meaning man or woman—all of mankind. The hidden person of the heart is the real you. In fact, your heart (the real you) is the seat of your moral activity, and it contains the root of your spiritual life.

Let me repeat that: Your heart is the seat of your moral activity, and it contains the root of your spiritual life.

5. Location of Spirit and Soul.

The word *heart* also means spirit and soul. It does not mean just the *soul,* or just the *spirit.* Your spirit and soul are connected by your conscience; your conscience is part of your heart.

For example, have you ever had your conscience bother you or have something weigh heavy on your conscience? You can actually feel it deep inside of you.

Consider these words by Peter and how his words affect the consciences of his listeners:

"Therefore let all the house of Israel know assuredly that God has made this Jesus, whom you crucified, both Lord and Christ."

Now when they heard this, they were cut to the heart, and said to Peter and the rest of the apostles, "Men and brethren, what shall we do?"

Acts 2:37

Their consciences cause them to feel "cut to the heart" because it is from the heart, or hidden man, that the conscience flows. Such is how we are able to repent. Continuing on with verse 38:

Then Peter said to them, "Repent, and let every one of you be baptized in the name of Jesus Christ for the remission of sins; and you shall receive the gift of the Holy Spirit."

Remember, a true disciple mourns with a godly sorrow for where he or she has erred or fallen short for the purpose of repentance.

What Else Flows from the Heart?

As we have learned, the conditions of your heart determine the issues of your life. What else flows out of your heart according to Scripture?

1. Sorrow flows from the Heart (II Cor. 2:4).

For I wrote you out of great sorrow and deep distress [with mental torture and anxiety] of heart, [yes, and] with many tears, not to cause you pain but in order to make you realize the overflowing love that I continue increasingly to have for you. (AMP)

2. Joy flows from the Heart (Eph. 5:19).

Speaking to yourselves in psalms and hymns and spiritual songs, singing and making melody in your heart to the Lord. (KJV)

3. Desire flows from the Heart (II Pet. 2:14).

Having eyes full of adultery and that cannot cease from sin, enticing unstable souls. They have a heart trained in covetous practices, and are accursed children.

4. Affections flow from the Heart (Luke 24:32).

Speaking of Jesus:

They said to one another, "Did not our heart burn within us while He talked with us on the road, and while He opened the Scriptures to us?"

5. Perceptions flow from the Heart (Eph. 4:18).

Having their understanding darkened, being alienated from the life of God, because of the ignorance that is in them, because of the blindness of their heart.

How you perceive life around you comes from the heart. It is not just what you hear or see, but it is your perception that has an impact on you.

6. Thoughts and Intentions flow from the Heart
(Matt. 9:4; Heb. 4:12).

Jesus, knowing their thoughts, said, "Why do you think evil in your hearts?" . . .

For the word of God is living and powerful, and sharper than any two-edged sword, piercing even to the division of soul and spirit, and of joints and marrow, and is a discerner of the thoughts and intents of the heart.

7. Understanding flows from the Heart (Matt. 13:15).

"For the hearts of this people have grown dull. Their ears are hard of hearing, and their eyes they have closed, lest they should see with their eyes and hear with their ears, lest they should understand with their hearts and turn, so that I should heal them."

8. Reasoning Powers flow from the Heart
(Mark 2:6, KJV).

But there were certain of the scribes sitting there, and reasoning in their hearts.

9. Imaginations flow from the Heart (Luke 1:51).

He has shown strength with His arm; He has scattered the proud in the imagination of their hearts.

10. Purpose flows from the Heart (II Cor. 9:7).

So let each one give as he purposes in his heart, not grudgingly or of necessity; for God loves a cheerful giver.

This Scripture is used all of the time with the giving of offerings; but, have you noticed that it says from where the purpose comes? The purpose flows from the heart.

11. Your Will flows from the Heart (Rom. 6:17).

But God be thanked that though you were slaves of sin, yet you obeyed from the heart that form of doctrine to which you were delivered.

12. Faith flows from the Heart (Mark 11:23; Rom. 10:10).

"For assuredly, I say to you, whoever says to this mountain, 'Be removed and be cast into the sea,' and does not doubt in his heart, but believes that those things he says will be done, he will have whatever he says."

For with the heart one believes unto righteousness, and with the mouth confession is made unto salvation.

A True Disciple is Pure in Heart

In the spiritual progression of a true disciple, Jesus says, "Blessed [happy, spiritually prosperous, and enjoying enviable favor] are you when you are poor in spirit (spiritually dependent), have a godly sorrow (mourning), yield your strength and authority to Me (meek), and hunger and thirst after Me, for then I will fill and satisfy you. In that fullness, you will be compassionate and merciful to those around you. As you demonstrate this love in action, you cleanse yourself and are single in purpose as you help others; not because it is required, but because it is WHO YOU ARE. It is your CHARACTER—it is purity of heart—you are PURE IN HEART."

Such is the progression of a true disciple; however, do not allow yourself to stumble at the *pure in heart* stage because of impure character blockers.

Character Impurities

The following are seven characteristics of an impure heart, or impurities in your character:

1. Self-Centeredness.

The first character blocker is being self-centered, which is a dedication to self and forgetting about others. There is an old saying that goes, "God bless me, my house, us four, and no more." This is not the character of a true disciple.

2. Laxity.

If you are lax in your attitude, or if you reject standards and authority, then you have impurities in your heart. They must be cleansed away.

3. Dishonesty.

This impurity is far too common. If you have to concentrate on telling the truth verses lying, then there is an impurity that needs to be fixed. Truth should flow out before any outside influence of a lie or hypocrisy. Dishonesty is associated with being oblivious to lying, deceit, and shadiness. If this type of sin is going on around you and you are just oblivious to it, then there are probably some impurities you need to cleanse out.

4. Distrust.

If you have a problem trusting people that you should normally be able to trust, and they have not given you a reason to distrust them, then you have some contaminates in your character. Maybe it is from being lied to in the past, but letting past hurts and fears go is part of the cleansing process.

5. Greed.

If you have a tendency to be greedy—if you are overly concerned that you are not going to receive your "fair share"—if you have an overwhelming desire to push through people at a convention to grab the front row seats, or fight to get in front of the line at the buffet table, then your heart may house some contaminates causing you to be greedy. Jesus says, *"But many that are first shall be last; and the last shall be first"* (Matt. 19:30, KJV).

Having difficulty turning over God's portion of your income to His storehouse could also indicate that you are struggling with greed. Clean that junk out! God will bless you more than you could ever hornswoggle for yourself.

6. Apathy.

If you lack interest in others—if you have an uncaring, unconcerned attitude, or if you are cool, aloof, and detached, then you could be apathetic. Do not let this condition linger on in our life. Cleanse yourself!

7. Irresponsibility.

If you are unreliable or lack accountability, then you could be called irresponsible. For example, if you tell your pastor that you will serve in a particular area at the church and then not show up because you either forgot or did not feel like helping after all, then you are unreliable. This is a character impurity that needs to be cleansed.

The Fact of the Matter

It does not matter if you go to church every Sunday wearing your best clothes and your best smile. If your heart is impure and contaminated with any of these character impurities, then Jesus says that you are a "pretender."

> *You blind Pharisee! First clean the inside of the cup and of the plate, so that the outside may be clean also.*
>
> *Woe to you, scribes and Pharisees, pretenders (hypocrites)! For you are like tombs that have been whitewashed, which look beautiful on the outside but inside are full of dead men's bones and everything impure.*
>
> *Just so, you also outwardly seem to people to be just and upright but inside you are full of pretense and lawlessness and iniquity.*

Matthew 23:26-28, AMP

Jesus is saying that when you look whitewashed, cleansed, and pure on the outside, and you have not done anything to cleanse your insides, then you are full of pretense, lawlessness, iniquity, and you are a hypocrite.

Wow! Those are harsh words. But, I believe Jesus means what He says. I am going to do my best to cleanse my heart of all impurities. Everyone striving to be a true disciple must do the same.

Being pure in heart is removing all that is tainted on the inside of you.

Jesus is saying that all the pretense and outward emotions of one's life amount to nothing if you are corrupt on the inside. Such will be burnt away, and all that will be left is what is on the inside of a person. In this case, it was bones.

> *Draw near to God and He will draw near to you. Cleanse your hands, you sinners; and purify your hearts, you double-minded.*
>
> James 4:8

Purity in its finest form is singleness of purpose. This Scripture says, *"purify your hearts, you double-minded."* In other words, get single-minded. Become of one mind toward God.

> *And may the Lord make you to increase and excel and overflow in love for one another and for all people, just as we also do for you. So that He may strengthen and confirm and establish your hearts faultlessly pure and unblamable in holiness in the sight of our God and Father, at the coming of our Lord Jesus Christ (the Messiah) with all His saints (the holy and glorified people of God)! Amen, (so be it)!*
>
> I Thessalonians 3:12-13, AMP

Being pure in heart is removing all that is tainted on the inside of you.

How to Stay Pure in Heart

Once cleansed, it is important to stay that way. One way to remain pure in heart is to choose your friends wisely.

Run from anything that stimulates youthful lusts
[not youthful in age, but in your walk]. *Instead,*
pursue righteous living, faithfulness, love, and peace.
Enjoy the companionship of those who call on the
Lord with pure hearts.

II Timothy 2:22, NLT

The friends with whom you associate will actually affect the purity of your heart. (Parents, this is good instruction for your children!) If you fellowship on a regular basis with people who have impure hearts then it will taint you. There is an expression, "One bad apple will spoil the barrel." It does not work the other way around. One good apple will not make the bad apples good, but a bad apple in the barrel will ruin the good ones.

Paul says to run from these associations. If you do not, you will find yourself with impure traits that will need to be cleansed. How can you tell if your companions have impure hearts? Well, are they single in purpose for God? If not, then you have your answer.

You might say, "If I use that gauge, I won't have any friends!" Well, that is not Bible either. The Word says that if you want to have friends, show yourself friendly (Prov. 18:24). However, choose wisely to whom you show yourself. The good news is that the remainder of that verse reads: *"There is a friend who sticks closer than a brother."*

So, if you do not have any friends in your life right now who are pure in heart, you can fellowship with Jesus. Then, trust Him to bring you new friends who have singleness in purpose for God. Going to church and associating with people with pure hearts is a great way to create friendships.

How else can you stay cleansed? The psalmist David says, by not lifting up your own desires or intentionally deceiving anyone.

> *Who may ascend into the hill of the Lord? Or who may stand in His holy place? He who has **clean hands** and **a pure heart**, who has not lifted up his soul to an idol ["vanity" KJV], nor sworn deceitfully.*
>
> Psalm 24:3-4

In other words, you cannot elevate your own desires to such a level of importance that they become an idol to you. The *King James Version* uses the word *vanity*. Noah Webster defines *vanity* as a "fruitless desire or endeavor" and "trifling labor that produces no good."

Have you ever found yourself thinking about your own desires that really amounted to nothing in the long run? David says that this is an impurity of the heart. Notice that he puts "exalting one's desires" on the same level as "lying and deceiving others." They are both self-serving, but our society does not see anything wrong with pleasing yourself. This could be a very deceptive contaminate if you do not closely monitor your moral and mental activity center, which is your heart.

Purification of the soul is a cleansing process that takes time.

Indeed, the purification of the soul is a cleansing process that takes time; however, you should become more pure in heart with each passing day. As true disciples, we will want to be among those without spot and blemish when our Lord Jesus appears to catch His righteous in the air (I Thess. 4:17). In order to do so, we must rid ourselves of any deceptive notion that we can associate with anyone we please or prop up our vanities without being tainted. Anyone who believes this to be true is self-deceived already, which is the highest form of deception.

We must be diligent to cleanse our hearts of all of these impurities. We must not put ourselves in a position to be deceived by those around us who are not single minded in purpose for the Lord.

Now, listen to me, I am not talking about being unkind or unloving to other people who are not living their lives in a single-minded purpose for the Lord. We still need to be an influence; HOWEVER, these people should not be your constant companions. Otherwise, they will negatively influence you.

God loves everyone, and He wants to use everyone. He wants to use those creative minds, and He can use us more often and more effectively for His kingdom when our hearts are pure. That means having a singleness of purpose, and singleness of your thoughts, mind, and heart for Him.

Out of the abundance of the heart the mouth speaks, but your thoughts proceed forth out of your heart, as do your imaginations and dreams. We must keep them pure.

I look at the young people in my congregation and know among them may be a future professional athlete, governor, mayor, doctor, lawyer, or business person. But, you know, the best thing that I could ever hear is if one of them wants to be a preacher. Wow! That means someone is living the right life around them.

Jesus says, "Blessed are those with a singleness of purpose in their innermost being; they have cleansed the impurities from their heart. They are unmixed with no pretense. They are unmasked. They are pure in heart, and they will see God." Hallelujah!

CHAPTER 11

BLESSED ARE THE PEACEMAKERS

Blessed are the peacemakers,
for they shall be called sons of God.

—*Matthew 5:9*

By now, a life-altering change has occurred in the character of a true disciple. A spiritual progression has been made toward God, a filling has been given by the Father, and that filling has been turned toward the world. Now the disciple of Jesus Christ is merciful and single-minded in purpose for the Lord (pure in heart). The characteristic of being pure in heart brings us to the next progression, which is **peacemaker**.

You may be thinking, "What is a peacemaker, and what exactly is a peacemaker supposed to do?" These questions can only be answered if you understand the nature or character of a peacemaker.

Remember, we are dealing with a spiritual progression (Matt. 5:3-12). You do not just jump into being a peacemaker without first being merciful (verse 7), and you cannot be merciful without first being poor in spirit (verse 3). Jesus lays out a spiritual progression, and not a random checklist of things a disciple should be and do. Jesus removes all the guesswork and gives us a foolproof plan of how to develop the character of a true disciple and walk in the blessing—and it occurs through a spiritual progression.

Once you have the characteristics of verses 3 through 8 flowing in your life (spiritually dependent, mourning unto godly sorrow, meekness, hungering and thirsting for righteousness, merciful, and pure in heart), Jesus says you are ready to become a peacemaker.

The word *peacemaker* comes from a very unusual Greek word *eirenopoios*, which means "not contentious or quarrelsome."

Peacemakers are Not Quarrelsome

Have you ever known anyone who just likes to quarrel? You may try to discuss something with them, but they end up quarrelling with you? It is as if they argue just to hear themselves argue.

Tenacious arguers are sometimes called ornery and mean-spirited, but I do not believe that is always the case. Some people are just prone to argue more than others. However, when it comes to dedicated disciples of Jesus Christ, I believe their desire to argue indicates where they are in their character walk or spiritual progression. I am not trying to put anyone down, but you have to understand, THIS IS WHAT I AM TRYING TO FIX!

If someone on the path of true discipleship is quarrelsome by nature, then developing the character of a peacemaker will require making peace with that tendency. However, true disciples who have genuinely progressed through being *pure in heart* do not even want to argue any more. Why? Because they have had a character change. They have been in the presence of the Lord hungering and thirsting after righteousness. They have reached out and started to help people, and they are single in their purpose of serving the Lord. They are pure in heart. Disciples who are pure in heart no longer have it in their nature to argue.

"Blessed are the peacemakers, for they shall be called sons of God."

> **The world will recognize the presence of the Lord on you.**

Notice this verse does not say that God calls peacemakers the sons of God. No, it says, *"they shall be **called** sons of God."* People of the world will recognize the presence of the Lord on you as you walk in peace. However, this does not happen when you are quarrelsome. You are called "sons of God" when you are blessed with being a peacemaker.

Peacemakers are Free from Strife

The Greek word e*irenopoios* also means "free from strife or disorder." I do not know about you, but when I get home from church, meetings, or wherever, I want my home and family to be peaceful. When a home is free from strife and disorder, there is peace, which is so much better than coming home to contention.

The Greek word also means "quiet." Have you heard the phrase "peace and quiet?" In the Greek, both are the same word.

Eirenopoios also means "free from disquieting thoughts or emotions." Do you ever have thoughts that are disturbing or experience emotions that are unsettling? If so, then you need to be the peacemaker in your emotions and thought life.

Peace Must Be Made

Let us break down the Greek word *eirenopoios* further. The first part comes from the word *eirene,* which means "peace," and the second part comes from the word *poieo,* which is translated "to make." The implication in the Greek that cannot be overlooked is that you are "blessed" because you MAKE peace. Peace does not just happen. That is why I call our military people and law enforcement "BLESSED." They are in the business of making peace.

When I was young, I used to enjoy watching old western movies. I liked all the bang 'em up shootouts and the bad guys being brought to justice. Now, those stories were mostly fiction, but there was some truth to them. For instance, the bad guys generally outnumbered the town sheriff and his deputies, which made it difficult to "keep the peace" in certain areas.

As a result, a gun manufacturer by the name of Colt made a revolver that could shoot six rounds of ammunition, which was very high-tech in those days. Although originally made for the U.S. Cavalry, this gun was provided to law enforcement or "peace officers." The gun was aptly named the **Colt Peacemaker**, and it did not take long for the outlaws to start avoiding the peace officers who carried this gun. My point is that peace did not come on its own, rather peace had to be made, and often by force.

Our military has the mission of making peace, and they are blessed because they are operating for God, country, and duty. Some say, "But, our military is fighting and killing!" No, that is not what they want to do; they just want to make peace. Yes, there may be some fighting to bring that peace about, but their goal is to make peace.

What about us? Once we arrive at the peacemaker stage in our progression, how are we supposed to go about making peace? Are we to walk around with a Colt Peacemaker strapped to our hip and make peace? No, that is probably not the type of peacemaking most disciples are called to do unless in the military or law enforcement. For most of us, the peacemaking we are to be involved in lies in the area of making peace through reconciliation, with emphasis on reconciling God to man through Jesus Christ.

Our working definition of *peacemaker* is one who makes peace by reconciliation.

Peace by Reconciliation

The highest standard of peace by reconciliation was set by the Lord Jesus Christ. Jesus died for the sins of mankind; He reconciled mankind with the Father. Jesus was born to bring peace by reconciliation, and He is the Prince of Peace (Isa. 9:6).

According to Paul, we are also given the ministry of reconciliation. Speaking of Jesus' crucifixion, Paul writes to the church in Corinth:

For the love of Christ compels us, because we judge thus: that if One died for all, then all died; and He died for all, that those who live should live no longer for themselves, but for Him who died for them and rose again.

Therefore, from now on, we regard no one according to the flesh. Even though we have known Christ according to the flesh, yet now we know Him thus no longer.

Therefore, if anyone is in Christ, he is a new creation; old things have passed away; behold, all things have become new.

*Now all things are of God, who has reconciled us to Himself through Jesus Christ, and has given us the **ministry of reconciliation**, that is, that God was in Christ reconciling the world to Himself, not imputing their trespasses to them, and has committed to us the **word of reconciliation.***

Now then, we are ambassadors for Christ, as though God were pleading through us: we implore you on Christ's behalf, be reconciled to God. For He made Him who knew no sin to be sin for us, that we might become the righteousness of God in Him.

II Corinthians 5:14-21

According to *Vine's*, the word *reconciliation* comes from the Greek word *katallage*, and indicates the "beseeching of men to be reconciled to God on the ground of what God has wrought in Christ."

> *Jesus is the ultimate peacemaker.*

Through Jesus Christ, we are reconciled with God the Father. This makes Jesus the ULTIMATE PEACE-MAKER! This is the good news of the Gospel! Man has been reconciled to God through Jesus Christ. As true disciples, we are to share this good news to the world; thus, the ministry of reconciliation!

Further, according to *Vine's*, the word *reconciliation* also means "the change on the part of one party, induced by the action on the part of another." So, another facet of our assignment is to make peace by reconciliation between two parties using Jesus as our example.

According to Noah Webster, *reconciliation* means "the act of reconciling parties at variance, or the renewal of friendship after disagreement or enmity." It also means "to restore to friendship or harmony."

An extremely important demonstration of peacemaking is in the home. If there is disharmony in the home, it is vital that the parties reconcile because a person's home life is an everyday encounter. Strife and contention in the home will wear on you and affect all the other areas in your life.

As true disciples, we are to make peace with the ultimate goal of reconciliation, which is what Paul demonstrates in his letter to the Corinthians that we just read. In that letter, Paul reveals that without Jesus Christ, we are all at odds with the Father; we are in strife and disorder—not reconciled together. Paul is about the ministry of reconciliation.

Additionally, Paul's letter reveals eight requirements to be a peacemaker. Did you catch them? Those requirements are: (1) being free of self; (2) not overly sensitive; (3) not touchy; (4) not on the defensive; (5) not one to sacrifice truth for peace; (6) not one to make peace at any cost; (7) not an appeaser, and (8) one who remains in the presence of the Lord. Let us look at these requirements of a peacemaker in more detail:

Peacemakers are Free of Self

The first characteristic of a peacemaker is being free from *yourself*. For instance, if your reason for reconciling two people is for your benefit, then you have missed the entire step of being in the presence of the Lord. Your desire to reconcile others should stem from Jesus reconciling you to God.

In order to be a peacemaker, you have to free yourself from your own self. Why? Because you want to reconcile people to God, not to you.

There are people who reconcile people to themselves and believe everything is fine. However, that is not peace at all.

That is setting up your own little kingdom, and the next thing you know, if anyone touches it, there is no peace. The result is drama and contention.

You must genuinely be free from self so that you can reconcile people to God, not to you. You might say, "Well, what if they need reconciling to me?" Then you should not be so easily offended. You should be a forgiver so that there is no need for someone to have to reconcile themselves to you.

Peacemakers Keep Emotions in Check

To be a peacemaker, you must not be overly sensitive, touchy, or defensive. Peacemakers keep their emotions in check.

Paul speaks about this in First Corinthians:

Love suffers long and is kind; love does not envy; love does not parade itself, is not puffed up; does not behave rudely, does not seek its own, is not provoked, thinks no evil.

I Corinthians 13:4-5

How grateful we are that Jesus was not overly sensitive and touchy! If He were ultrasensitive, He could have called a legion of angels down and destroyed all who opposed Him; however, if such were the case, we would not have the precious gift of salvation. If Jesus were touchy, He would have destroyed half of His disciples before completing His earthly assignment.

If you are overly sensitive and touchy about everything, then I have some good news and bad news for you. The good news is that you will never have to worry about becoming a peacemaker. The bad news is that your spiritual progression will stagnate at the peacemaker stage, thus hindering your blessings when faced with the issues of life.

I have never seen a time when Christians were as sensitive and touchy as in this day and hour—and I am talking about Christians who should be mature. Do you know someone who is overly sensitive and touchy? I am assuming it is not you. If it is you, then God has you in the right place. Hallelujah! He loves you and wants you to mature so you can walk in the blessings.

What about being on the defensive? The world will tell you that you have to look out for yourself first, right? Wrong! We have our heavenly Father looking out for our interests. That is part of the benefit of walking in the character of the blessed!

Peacemakers are not on the defensive.

Peacemakers are not on the defensive. Do you know what I mean by that? It is to feel the need to defend yourself. It is an attitude of protecting yourself first and living for yourself. In Second Corinthians 5:15, Paul instructs, *"those who live should live no longer for themselves."*

If every time God tries to use you, you end up getting on the defensive, then you cannot operate as the blessed peacemaker you need to be. Why? Because a true disciple ministering from the presence of God, whose singleness of purpose is peace by reconciliation, cannot afford to be on the defensive!

In fact, let me give you a little key to help you. Have you ever had the Devil try to tell you that you are not really saved? The first time you missed the mark you heard, "See, you aren't really saved. If you were, then you wouldn't have said that."

You see, Satan is a thief, and a thief comes to steal, kill, and destroy; HOWEVER, he cannot steal something you DO NOT have. The very fact that he tries to steal from you means there is something you have that can be stolen.

Alright, now flip that around, and take this as a sign: If you find yourself getting on the defensive, that is proof that God wants to move you into a peacemaker. Think about it. If you did not have the choice to make peace, then the Devil could not steal it from you. The moment you begin to get on the defensive is the moment you have the choice to *make peace* instead.

So, the first time you catch yourself becoming defensive, say to yourself, "Whoa, stop! That is my sign that I'm right here at the peacemaker stage. And the Devil is trying to steal something I have and put me on the defense." Let that be your trigger that you are almost there.

Peacemakers Do Not Compromise

Let me take a moment to interject an important aspect of peacemaking. As a peacemaker, when you are about the ministry of reconciliation in your daily walk, it is important to remember that the peace you make must be *true peace*. How do you determine true peace? True peace is based on truth—the truth of God's Word, and you must never sacrifice that truth to make peace.

1. Peacemakers Do Not Sacrifice Truth for Peace.

True peace is based on truth with no room for compromise. By compromise, I am not talking about minor issues such as where to set the thermostat, or at which restaurant to eat. What I am talking about is bowing, backing down, and changing the truth. You must never sacrifice truth even if the result is peace.

True peace reconciles, but it does not compromise; therefore, there is a price to be paid for true peace. It will cost you. It cost Jesus His life. If you are going to be a peacemaker, then you cannot compromise the truth.

There is a saying, "What you compromise to keep you will eventually lose." I will tell you right now that I have lost a lot of people and things because of compromising while thinking I was keeping peace.

Further, a peacemaker must not sacrifice something of importance just to make peace. The ministry of reconciliation is not "peace at any cost." Such leaves the potential for resentment and bitterness to develop.

2. Peacemakers Do Not Engage in Peace at Any Cost.

What about appeasing or pacifying someone? Is that okay if it will keep the peace? Well, let me ask you. Have you ever had someone say something to you just to appease you, but you knew good and well they did not give a hoot about what you were saying? It did not make you feel too good, did it?

Peace achieved by appeasing is not based on truth; it is just smoothing something over on the surface. Such peace is a counterfeit and will not last. It is false peace, and it can destroy people because it is not based on truth.

3. Peacemakers are Not Appeasers.

If you are going to be a peacemaker, you need to make up your mind right now that you are not going to be an appeaser. Appeasing is counterfeit peacemaking.

Some may say, "If I just tell the truth, then I am not sure anyone will want to listen to me." Well, that is okay because as a peacemaker, you have peace. And with peace comes *"perfect well-being, all necessary good, all spiritual prosperity, and freedom from fears and agitating passions and moral conflicts"* (II Pet. 1:2, AMP). When people come to you, they will say, "This person must be a son of God because he has peace around him."

Peacemakers Walk in the Atmosphere of God

The reason peacemakers are called "sons of God" is because they come out of the presence of the Lord with an atmosphere of peace. They bring a filling and a character of being merciful and pure in heart to their ministry of reconciliation, which is necessary because an atmosphere of peace reveals the internal wars of others.

Read these words of the prophet Isaiah:

"For the iniquity of his covetousness I was angry and struck him; I hid and was angry, and he went on backsliding in the way of his heart.

"I have seen his ways, and will heal him; I will also lead him, and restore comforts to him and to his mourners.

"I create the fruit of the lips: Peace, peace to him who is far off and to him who is near," says the LORD, "And I will heal him."

But the wicked are like the troubled sea, when it cannot rest, whose waters cast up mire and dirt.

"There is no peace," says my God, "for the wicked."

Isaiah 57:17-21

When you are a peacemaker, with a singleness of purpose, love, and compassion coming from the presence of God, it will cause people to want to be around you because you are godly. They will want the peace you have. An ungodly person cannot be a peacemaker because they are only interested in peace on their own terms.

As we see from this passage in Isaiah, when God is the source of the peace, it is peace that heals. People who are not at peace with God cannot be at peace with themselves or others.

True peace can exist in the middle of trials and tribulation.

Do you know why most peace talks do not work? First, because they are trying to reconcile with each other. If they would reconcile with God, they could find a solution.

Secondly, they are trying to find peace through contention and agitation. True peace cannot be found through agitation.

"There is no peace," says my God, "for the wicked."

True peace can only come when God is involved in a person's life. True peace comes through Jesus Christ who reconciled God to man. The world has no peace to offer. Jesus says,

Peace I bequeath to you, my own peace I give you, a peace which the world cannot give, this is my gift to you.

John 14:27, NJB

For the godly, true peace can exist in the middle of trials and tribulation through our Lord Jesus Christ.

I have told you all this so that you may find peace in me. In the world you will have hardship, but be courageous: I have conquered the world.

John 16:33, NJB

True peace exists for peacemakers who face the issues of life with a confident attitude; they are not easily offended or quick to stumble. Remember, true disciples adhere to the teaching of the Word.

Great peace have they who love Your law; nothing shall offend them or make them stumble.

Psalm 119:165, AMP

What have we discovered about true peace?

- True peace is based on the truth and does not compromise.
- True peace comes from a relationship with God so there can be reconciliation.
- True peace does not come out of agitation.
- True peace can exist in the middle of tribulation and trials.
- Peacemakers have a confident attitude because they do not become offended, and they do not stumble.

Rewards for the Peacemaker

"Blessed are the peacemakers, for they shall be called sons of God."

The first reward for being a peacemaker is being called a son of God. Secondly, you will walk in peace because peace is the fruit of righteousness.

Now the fruit of righteousness is sown in peace by those who make peace.

James 3:18

The New Jerusalem Bible translation reads:

The peace sown by peacemakers brings a harvest of justice.

Finally, by being a peacemaker, you overcome evil by doing good. Recall the passage in Romans chapter 12 that we studied in relation to being merciful. The theme is doing good, even to your enemies.

"If your enemy is hungry, feed him; if he is thirsty, give him a drink; for in so doing you will heap coals of fire on his head."

Do not be overcome by evil, but overcome evil with good.

In addition to being merciful, doing good to your enemies demonstrates your character as a peacemaker. By overcoming evil by doing good, you cause others to reconcile with the Lord, and such is the ultimate fulfillment in your ministry of reconciliation.

As a true disciple, if you want to walk blessed in life, you need to be one who makes peace by reconciling people to God—a peacemaker. In addition, if you have peace working in your life as a blessed character trait, I can promise you that it will cause difficulties in your life to seem insignificant in comparison. Why? Because you have peace—and it is a peace that transcends our understanding (Phil. 4:7).

CHAPTER 12

BLESSED ARE THOSE WHO ARE PERSECUTED . . . FOR GREAT IS YOUR REWARD

BLESSED ARE THOSE WHO ARE PERSECUTED FOR RIGHTEOUSNESS' SAKE, FOR THEIRS IS THE KINGDOM OF HEAVEN. BLESSED ARE YOU WHEN THEY REVILE AND PERSECUTE YOU, AND SAY ALL KINDS OF EVIL AGAINST YOU FALSELY FOR MY SAKE. REJOICE AND BE EXCEEDINGLY GLAD, FOR GREAT IS YOUR REWARD IN HEAVEN, FOR SO THEY PERSECUTED THE PROPHETS WHO WERE BEFORE YOU.

—MATTHEW 5:10-12

Up to this point, we have experienced a spiritual progression toward God (poor in spirit, mourning, meekness, and hunger and thirsting for righteousness), and then a spiritual progression toward mankind (merciful, pure in heart, and peacemaker). Such a progression takes perseverance, self-control, and a singleness of purpose, which are all traits of a true disciple of Jesus Christ.

We have found that as you deal with the issues of life as a true disciple, first of all, YOU ARE ABUNDANTLY BLESSED. However, once you have all seven of the characteristics of a true disciple operating in your life, you arrive at the next progression, which is **persecution**.

Persecution is not a subject most Christians like to hear about.

Persecution is not a subject most Christians like to hear about, yet here we are at its doorstep in our spiritual progression.

168

What Does Persecution Mean?

The word *persecution* in the Greek is *dioko*, which means "to put to flight, to drive away, to pursue, to chase away, to harass, and to treat evilly." It does NOT mean sickness, disease, calamity, catastrophe, or financial problems. The result of those things may feel like persecution, but Jesus' use of the word *persecution* in Matthew means "to drive away."

Have you ever known, beyond a shadow of a doubt, that something you were doing was God's will? When you know you are in God's will, the enemy's best weapon is to cause people to try to drive you away from that will. Such is persecution.

You do not get persecuted because you accepted the Lord thirty years ago and have never done much more than go to church on Sunday mornings. You do not get persecuted because you say you are a Christian. No, you get persecuted when you live in the character of the blessed; you get persecuted when you decide to be a disciple and develop your character so that you are poor in spirit, mournful for past mistakes, meek, hungry and thirsty for righteousness, merciful, pure in heart, and a peacemaker.

Anytime you dedicate yourself to become a true disciple, Jesus says the result is persecution.

Jesus differentiates two origins of persecution: first, persecution for *righteousness' sake*, which could come from other Christians, family members, or friends, and second,

> *You will be blessed when you are persecuted for living godly.*

persecution for *Jesus' sake*, which comes primarily from the world. In other words, there is persecution for living godly ("righteousness' sake"), and for serving Jesus ("My sake"). In short, when you walk in the character of the blessed, you will be persecuted for how you live and who you live for.

PERSECUTION FOR RIGHTEOUSNESS' SAKE

"Blessed are those who are persecuted for righteousness' sake, for theirs is the kingdom of heaven."

Matthew 5:10

As we discovered earlier, the word *righteousness* comes from the Greek word *dikaiosune*, which means "the character or quality of being right or just" or "rightwiseness." *Young's* translates *dikaiosune* simply as "rightness."

Jesus is saying, "Blessed are those who are persecuted for **rightness**." In other words, you will be blessed when you are persecuted for **living godly**.

Persecution or Compromise?

You may be thinking, "Now, Pastor Billy, I don't walk in all of the characteristics of a true disciple, but I'm still being persecuted. Why is that?"

If you are not walking in the character of the blessed, and you feel you are being persecution, then your persecution comes as a result of *compromise*. What?

Hear me, now. I am here to tell you that most of the persecution Christians suffer in life comes as the result of compromise, not because they are walking in the character of the blessed. When you get serious and start walking in the blessings of a true disciple and persecution comes, it will be because of a *non-compromising* Christian walk.

Why Not Just the Blessing?

Some Christians may ask, "Well, why is it that if I'm poor in spirit, have a godly sorrow, yield my strength to the Lord, hunger and thirst after righteousness, am love in action, have singleness of mind and purpose, and am a peacemaker, then why will my development end up in persecution instead of just the blessing?"

The blessing WILL BE predominant in your life, but you will also suffer persecution for living godly. HOWEVER, let your persecution come from living godly—for righteousness' sake—and not for living like the world in compromise.

Consider the uncompromising nature of Moses:

> *By faith Moses, when he became of age, refused to be called the son of Pharaoh's daughter, choosing rather to suffer affliction with the people of God . . .*

The words *"suffer affliction with the people of God"* is not talking about sickness, disease, destruction, or devastation. Rather, it is talking about persecution.

> *. . . choosing rather to suffer affliction with the people of God than to enjoy the passing pleasures of sin, esteeming the reproach of Christ greater riches than the treasures in Egypt; for he looked to the reward.*
>
> Hebrews 11:24-26

Remember, when you are persecuted, it says here that your reward is in heaven. Moses looked to that reward. He would rather suffer persecution with the people of God than enjoy the pleasures of Egypt, the world, and sin.

In fact, most Christians are persecuted because they live a life of *compromise*. I am not trying to be mean when I say that.

I can look back at instances in my own life of compromise. Even when I had good intentions, I often compromised because I wanted to help in some way. The compromise was not sinful; it was in the area of certain decisions, rules, and regulations. I found out the hard way that if I compromised the littlest bit, even if it appeared that I had favor for a short while, ultimately it would not end well.

Anything you compromise to keep, you will eventually lose.

Persecution by the Flesh

As a believer, you not only have persecution for righteousness' sake, but if you do not watch out, your own flesh will persecute you. Your own flesh will persecute your spirit. Why is that? Because your spirit man has been made new.

> *Therefore, if anyone is in Christ, he is a new creation; old things have passed away; behold, all things have become new.*
>
> II Corinthians 5:17

Although your spirit man has been made new, you have to renew your mind and transform your thinking and thought process.

> *And do not be conformed to this world, but be transformed by the renewing of your mind, that you may prove what is that good and acceptable and perfect will of God.*
>
> Romans 12:2

Another factor you will have to contend with as you renew your mind is your physical body. How? Your physical body is still going to fight you because your flesh likes to be *pampered*. It is the truth!

All I would have to do at my church is turn off the air conditioning and many bodies would feel persecuted. Now, our church is out in the California desert heat, so I would not do that willfully, but you get my point. Our flesh, particularly here in the United States, is used to being pampered and getting its way.

Consider the teaching of Paul:

> *The Scriptures say that Abraham had two sons,
> one from his slave wife and one from his freeborn
> wife. The son of the slave wife* [Hagar] *was born **in a
> human attempt** to bring about the fulfillment of
> God's promise . . .*

Galatians 4:22-23, NLT

In other words, Abraham got into the flesh. Sarah offered
Abraham her hand maid, Hagar, to bear him a son because
Sarah did not understand in the natural how she could
conceive a child. Instead of depending on the promise of
God, Abraham took Hagar in an attempt to fulfill God's
promise himself.

> *But the son of the freeborn wife* [Sarah] *was born
> as God's own fulfillment of his promise.*

> *These two women serve as an illustration of God's
> two covenants. The first woman, Hagar, represents
> Mount Sinai where people received the law that
> enslaved them. And now Jerusalem is just like Mount
> Sinai in Arabia, because she and her children live in
> slavery to the law. But the other woman, Sarah, repre-
> sents the heavenly Jerusalem. She is the free woman,
> and she is our mother.*

> *As Isaiah said, "Rejoice, O childless woman, you
> who have never given birth! Break into a joyful shout,
> you who have never been in labor! For the desolate*

174

woman now has more children than the woman who lives with her husband!"

And you, dear brothers and sisters, are children of the promise, just like Isaac. But you are now being persecuted by those who want you to keep the law, just as Ishmael, the child born by human effort, persecuted Isaac, the child born by the power of the Spirit.

Galatians 4:23-29, NLT

What Paul is saying is that there is a constant war going on in you, and that constant war is your flesh battling your spirit. You must begin a Word-oriented walk. You must get the characteristics of the blessing in your life and make a stand to crucify the flesh. If not, your own flesh will persecute your spirit. Your own carnal body will fight against that which is spiritual. The proof can be seen when you just leave your flesh alone, and watch what it does. Your own flesh will war with your spirit.

> *Your own carnal body will fight against that which is spiritual.*

Although most Christians suffer persecution because of compromise, many cause their own persecution by walking in the flesh. Have you ever heard the expression, "He or she is their own worst enemy?" We generally want to blame someone else for our shortcomings. Many want to blame their pastors for their problems. I cannot even count the number of times people have wanted to blame me for their problems.

But, I am here to tell you that most Christian's problems are because of compromise and walking in the flesh.

PERSECUTION FOR JESUS' SAKE

"Blessed are you when they revile and persecute you, and say all kinds of evil against you falsely for My sake."

Matthew 5:11

Once you have established the character to face persecution for righteousness' sake, and such persecution does not move you from your singleness in purpose for God, your mercy, or your peace, then you will progress to persecution for Jesus' sake. In this verse, Jesus is speaking of the world persecuting you.

In fact, you do not have to do a thing wrong, but the world will revile you, persecute you, say evil things and lie about you, simply because you are a disciple of Jesus and you walk in the blessings. Jesus says this persecution comes because of Him.

The word *revile* in the Greek is *oneidizo*, which means "to reproach or upbraid." *Webster's New Collegiate Dictionary* defines *reproach* as "to blame, discredit, or disgrace," and *upbraid* as "to criticize severely." Further, *Webster's* defines *revile* as "to subject to verbal abuse" and "to use abusive language."

We have already learned that *persecution* in the Greek means to put to flight or drive away.

Wow! That paints quite an ugly picture. Jesus is saying, "Blessed are you when they verbally abuse you with abusive language, blame you, discredit you, disgrace you, and criticize you severely in an attempt to run you off!"

Why Persecution Comes

There are many ways others are provoked to persecute you when you are a true disciple of Jesus Christ. But remember, it is Satan and his cohorts who are the source behind the persecution.

For we wrestle not against flesh and blood, but against principalities, against powers, against the rulers of the darkness of this world, against spiritual wickedness in high places.

Ephesians 6:12, KJV

We have seen in the Word that living godly ("righteousness sake") and serving Jesus ("My sake") are the two primary origins of persecution. We have also seen that when you walk in the characteristics of a true disciple, you are blessed with the blessings associated with that walk. Such is a reason for persecution.

1. Persecution comes because of the blessing.

As a true disciple, yours is the kingdom of heaven, you are comforted, you inherit the earth, you are filled by God, you obtain mercy, you see God, and you are called a son of

God. You enjoy the favor of God as you deal with the issues of life. Unfortunately, once you reach this stage, many of those around you do not take kindly to seeing you blessed to such a degree, particularly when they face many of the same issues without any blessings at all! I am talking about the world AND other Christians. Remember, not all Christians are true disciples.

When your character becomes blessed, the world envies you, but it is not a good envy—it is not the enviable favor that causes people to ask about your blessed life and how they may partake in the blessings of God themselves. No, this envy is demonic and associated with hatred.

But if ye have bitter envying and strife in your hearts, glory not, and lie not against the truth. This wisdom descendeth not from above, but is earthly, sensual, devilish. For where envying and strife is, there is confusion and every evil work.

James 3:14-16, KJV

When you walk in the blessing, the world will hate you and make up lies about you because of bitter envying that is sensual and devilish.

For we ourselves were also once foolish, disobedient, deceived, serving various lusts and pleasures, living in malice and envy, hateful and hating one another.

Titus 3:3

I know that sounds really bad, but Jesus says that you will be BLESSED as you face these situations in your everyday life for His sake. Remember, you are walking in the CHARACTER OF THE BLESSED!

"Blessed are you when they revile and persecute you, and say all kinds of evil against you falsely for My sake."

Matthew 5:11

Notice Jesus does not say, "Blessed are those when *maybe, perhaps, or occasionally* you might get persecuted." No, Jesus says, *"Blessed are you **when** they revile and persecute you."*

If you are going to serve Jesus and live godly, you are going to have to face the fact that persecution will come. I cannot even tell you the number of people who have spread false things about me and my church!

For example, years ago, we had an Assembly of God group called the Royal Rangers and Missionettes bring their program to our children's church. Now, we are not Assembly of God, but we thought they had a good program. If you have never heard of them, the Royal Rangers provide an adventure and character building program much like the Boy Scouts; the Missionettes provide the same type of program for girls.

One night, the Royal Rangers brought in animals as part of their program. A few days later, word spread around that we were a bunch of snake handlers. And people believed it!

If you have a pet snake, then that is between you and God, but I do not like snakes. And I certainly would not be handling them in church!

Well, when I wanted to get upset and go to source of it, something Bro. Copeland taught me kept resounding in my head: *If you go to spending your time defending yourself, that is all you will have time to do.*

So, the Lord led me to this: "Blessed are you when they speak falsely or say evil things about you."

I just had to consider my church blessed instead of getting upset and trying to defend myself. Now, I wanted to defend myself, but I did not.

God will bless you as you walk in the blessing, but the world will hate you for it. People will start making up reasons as to why you are blessed. They do not understand the principle of seedtime and harvest, or that walking in the blessing during seedtime causes a harvest. Because they do not understand godly principles, they assume your increase must come in the same way theirs would come if they were to be so blessed—either from the lottery or illegally. I could go on and on. But really, none of that matters, because Jesus gives us verse 12:

"Rejoice and be exceedingly glad, for great is your reward in heaven, for so they persecuted the prophets who were before you."

2. Persecution comes to cause you to compromise.

Recall, *persecution* in the Greek means "to drive away." Almost all persecution is designed to drive you away from that which you believe. If the world can get you away from what you believe, then that is called **compromise**. Again, we see that word!

Almost all persecution is designed to drive you away from that which you believe.

Changing what you believe or making alterations to what you believe is compromise. Do you maintain your principles even in the face of pressures, situations, or people? If so, then you have withstood persecution. Good for you! However, if not, then you compromised. It is that simple. Just repent and get back on God's will. That is simple, too!

3. Persecution comes for the Word's sake.

Jesus is the Word made flesh.

> *The Word became flesh and dwelt among us, and we beheld His glory, the glory as of the only begotten of the Father, full of grace and truth.*

> John 1:14

When persecution comes for the Word's sake, it is the same as it coming for Jesus' sake. Recall, our working definition of *persecution* from the Greek is nothing more than "that which drives you away." When you receive the Word of God and faith becomes activated, Satan comes to drive you away from what you have learned.

And these are they by the way side, where the word is sown; but when they have heard, Satan cometh immediately, and taketh away the word that was sown in their hearts.

Mark 4:15, KJV

The goal is to get you off of what you believe so that the Word has no effect in your life.

And have no root in themselves, and so endure but for a time: afterward, when affliction or persecution ariseth for the word's sake, immediately they are offended.

Mark 4:17, KJV

The *New Living Translation* interprets Jesus' words this way:

But since they don't have deep roots, they don't last long. They fall away as soon as they have problems or are persecuted for believing God's word.

If you are walking as a true disciple of Jesus Christ, then persecution comes for the Word's sake to get you off of your godly assignment; it is an attempt to move you from believing God's Word. It is called *compromise*, and it is a primary reason for persecution. If the Devil and his cohorts can move you into compromise, then the persecution sent your way has succeeded.

4. Persecution comes as a result of conviction.

As a true disciple, you are a convicting source to another's conscience.

As a true disciple, you are a convicting source to another's conscience. When you walk in the Word, those around you who are not walking in the Word become convicted in their consciences.

> *They demonstrate that God's law is written in their hearts, for their own **conscience** and thoughts either accuse them or tell them they are doing right.*
>
> Romans 2:15, NLT

Being blessed and walking in the blessing does not necessarily include people loving you. In fact, it is quite the opposite. When the ungodly get around you, the blessing flowing from you pricks their conscience and convicts them. What are they convicted of?

First, the ungodly are convicted of **pride** because they resent any kind of superiority or the need for our Savior, Jesus Christ.

Second, they are convicted of **envy**. They envy you because you are about "doing good" as Jesus instructs. You are merciful, compassionate, pure in heart, and a peacemaker. You have the blessings of God on you. Remember, blessed means enjoying enviable favor. This makes them envy you, and they feel convicted. This is when you overcome evil by doing good (Rom. 12:21).

Third, you convict them of **malice**, which means to inflict pain on another, and sometimes out of sheer meanness. You are living a pure life. You would not intentionally inflict pain on anyone, and this convicts those who do.

> *To the pure [in heart and conscience] all things are pure, but to the defiled and corrupt and unbelieving nothing is pure; their very minds and **consciences** are defiled and polluted.*
>
> Titus 1:15, AMP

Persecution comes because you convict people's consciences. Have you ever noticed when you decide to live godly, some of the people that you thought were close, are not close anymore? There are two reasons for this: (1) Your actions have become weird to them, and (2) Being around you convicts them in their consciences, so they had rather not fellowship with you.

5. Persecution comes when you are aggressive.

When you walk as a true disciple, you not only convict others in their consciences, but to them, YOU become the aggressor. Sound strange? Have you ever noticed a blessed person walking in the anointing?

I love traveling overseas with Kenneth Copeland. I love being around him because he is not a passive believer. He is aggressive. For example, I recall when we traveled to the Philippines for the first time to minister. I was doing my job getting everything ready. Then, as Bro. Copeland and I were walking to our destination, if he saw someone who was demon possessed or demonized, he would almost take off in a RUN to lay hands on them. If they fell to the ground, man, he would be on top of them casting a devil out. I would just watch and think to myself, "Whoa! I'm going to make sure to walk holy around him. I don't want that to happen to me." Praise God for Bro. Copeland!

My point is that as you walk in the character of the blessed, you convict the consciences of those around you just by your presence and actions, but you also convict people because you are aggressive about the things of God. They come up all mealy-mouthed and talking negative around you, and you say, "STOP! You don't want me to agree with those negative words, do you? Instead, let me tell you what the Word says about your situation!"

All of a sudden, you become aggressive in your walk, and boy, I tell you what, the world does not think like that. They will persecute you for saying such things.

I believe if Jesus Himself appeared to some Christians and said, "I am going to give you the next thing you say out loud." Their response would be something like, "Ho, Ho, that tickles me to death."

We have got to watch our words. When you become a person of blessed character, you become aggressive and dangerous to demonized people. The Devil does not want his servants around you. You are going to get them born again, in church, turned onto the Word, tithing, and they will not be poor anymore. They are going to get all excited and cleaned up with no more depression or oppression. All of a sudden, you are aggressive.

By aggressive, I do not mean overbearing. No, it is just because you walk in the character of the blessed that causes you to be aggressive about the things of God. You have learned what works, and you want to share that with those around you. Because of that, you are a danger to demonized people because you turn their world upside down. This is one of the reasons the religious leaders wanted to kill Jesus.

> *Then the chief priests and the Pharisees gathered a council and said, "What shall we do? For this Man works many signs. If we let Him alone like this, everyone will believe in Him, and the Romans will come and take away both our place and nation."*
>
> John 11:47-48

The Pharisees are saying, "We've got to kill this man because He is turning everything upside down!"

A true disciple is a danger to demonized people, so guess what? You become a danger to the world because you turn their world upside down. If Christians would unite, we could turn our nation back to God. We could put God back into our schools and the court system. However, it would take us living an **uncompromised** Christian life to do so.

When you are aggressive for the things of God, you live godly.

When you are aggressive for the things of God, you live godly. You have a zeal for souls. You have an uncompromising rebuke for what is wrong and what is evil. Once your principles are based on the Word of God, you adhere to those principles at all cost. There is no compromise in your vocabulary.

How to Live Without Persecution

On the flip side, every one of us can escape persecution if we so choose. In fact, you can go through life without being persecution at all. Let me show you. Paul says,

> But you, Timothy, certainly know what I teach, and how I live, and what my purpose in life is. You know my faith, my patience, my love, and my endurance. You know how much persecution and suffering I have endured. You know all about how I was persecuted in Antioch, Iconium, and Lystra—but the Lord rescued me from all of it. Yes, and everyone

who wants to live a godly life in Christ Jesus will
suffer persecution.

II Timothy 3:10-12, NLT

Paul was persecuted for living godly. So, how do you escape persecution? Well, just stop living godly. Stop doing the things you know you should do. You will not be persecuted for righteousness' sake, nor walk in the blessing associated with doing so. In fact, if you stop living godly, the world will start loving you. Stop serving Jesus, stop walking in the Word, and you will no longer be persecuted for His sake either.

Of course, I am not advocating this approach, and this certainly is not the correct answer for someone reading a book about developing the character of the blessed. No, as true disciples we are not going to allow potential persecution to modify our conviction.

Yet, there are plenty of churches with services designed to make you so comfortable that your conviction fades away. Ultimate grace, politically correct, universalism, and seeker friendly are all labels for these types of churches with easy-going doctrines that require no conviction. In fact, in most cases, the conviction of the Holy Spirit is not even welcomed. Thus, they have no need to concern themselves with persecution from the world.

It is when you make the decision to the live the Word out of conviction and walk as a true disciple in the character of the blessed that Jesus Himself tells us that we will suffer persecution. There is no getting around it.

When you come to a church that is filled with people full of the Holy Ghost, the presence of God is almost tangible as you enter into worship and praise. You are taught the Word, and the Word matures you. Out of that maturity you decide to live godly and develop the character of the blessed. As you do so, the Holy Spirit will convict you in areas that need to be submitted to the Lord. When you are obedient, and you set that kind of atmosphere in your life, you will be different from the world. And, guess what, the world is NOT going to like you. In fact, the world will hate you. I did not say they would dislike you. No, according to Jesus, they will hate you.

Now, I know no one wants to be hated, including me. I want to be loved by everyone. But, if you are going to be hated, it ought to be because you are living as a true disciple of Jesus Christ. Be persecuted for His sake.

"These things I command you, that you love one another. If the world hates you, you know that it hated Me before it hated you.

"If you were of the world, the world would love its own. Yet because you are not of the world, but I chose you out of the world, therefore the world hates you.

"Remember the word that I said to you, 'A servant is not greater than his master.' If they persecuted Me,

they will also persecute you. If they kept My word,
they will keep yours also.

"But all these things they will do to you for My
name's sake, because they do not know Him who
sent Me."

John 15:17-21

Logically, you would think that if you lived your life
upright and godly that the world would reward you and think
you are the best thing next to chocolate cake. However, such
is not the case.

Godly Reaction to Persecution

Jesus says that if you operate in the character of the
blessed, persecution will come. Yet, your behavior will be
different from anyone else on the planet. You will not run
into a corner, cry, ball up, and ask why no one loves you. No,
your response will be mature and established on the Word
with no fear or retreat in mind. Jesus says,

"Peace I leave with you, My peace I give to you;
not as the world gives do I give to you. Let not your
heart be troubled, neither let it be afraid."

John 14:27

True disciples continue with their godly assignments
in the face of persecution with no fear.

Early in my Christian walk, I learned this very important phrase: *This too shall pass.* When things get tough and persecution comes for making a stand of no compromise, you must say to yourself, "I am a godly person. This too shall pass. I will continue to do good."

In order to face persecution with no fear, it is important to maintain a clear conscience. It is your conscience that tells you whether you are doing right or wrong. Paul says,

> *They demonstrate that God's law is written in their hearts, for their own conscience and thoughts either accuse them or tell them they are doing right . . . I always try to maintain a clear conscience before God and all people.*

Romans 2:15, Acts 24:16, NLT

There is a confidence that comes from knowing you are doing right, even in the face of persecution. That confidence allows you to stand strong. Therefore, it is important to maintain a clear conscience before God and man.

True disciples maintain a clear conscience and face persecution with confidence.

If your conscience accuses you of doing wrong, your heart will condemn you.

However, if your conscience accuses you of doing wrong, your heart will condemn you. Recall from our study that your conscience dwells in your heart.

Beloved, if our heart condemn us not, then have we confidence toward God.

I John 3:21, KJV

You cannot stand confident toward God, or in your godly assignment, if your heart condemns you. Nor can you pray in faith to the Father. We all have had our conscience advise us of wrong doing, and we want that to continue when we are in error or "miss it" on occasion.

Lester Sumrall said that he did not like the word *mistake.* He said, "To my knowledge, I have never made a mistake." People would respond, "Huh?" He would quickly continue, "Now, I have missed it sometimes because of a lack of knowledge, but I straightened that out with prayer and repentance. So, it wasn't a mistake, I just missed it in that area."

Dr. Sumrall further explained that a mistake is when you know something is wrong, and you do it anyway. Some Christians may believe they are being persecuted when, in fact, they are being punished for knowingly doing something wrong. They are not punished by God, but by man. Persecution comes from doing good. Punishment comes from doing evil. There is a difference between the two.

When punishment comes, repentance is required for doing wrong. Conversely, persecution comes as a result of making a non-compromising stand.

In life, there will be people around you who knowingly do wrong, and there are people, including you, who are going to miss it on occasion; however, when you do, make sure to keep a clear conscience.

You may ask, "Well, if I miss it or do wrong, how can I keep a clear conscience?" You repent in a godly manner after godly sorrow—not because somebody caught you, but because you are sorry to God. This will keep your conscience clear. You purge it as dead works and sprinkle it with the blood of Christ.

> *But if we walk in the light, as He is in the light, we have fellowship with one another, and the **blood of Jesus Christ** His Son cleanseth us from all sin.*
>
> I John 1:7, KJV

Taking communion is the perfect point-of-faith opportunity to clear your conscience and purge dead works from your life. It is a time to be empowered, and not something you wait to do when everything is going well.

As a little boy, I did not go to church much, but when I did, I slept under the pew. If I moved or made any noise, I would get pinched or told I was going to "get it" when I got home. And I did! So, I learned it was best just to sleep, which became my idea of church—sleeping under the pew.

My impression of communion was that if I had been bad, I could not partake of it, which was about every time communion was offered. Now, I was not a mean kid; I was actually a very good kid, but I was not a Christian kid.

My point is that I thought communion was something that could only be taken if I was good. Once I got into the ministry, I realized communion is not something you set aside for when you have it all together. Communion is taken to remember the blood to purge your conscience. Then, you are able to get it together through the power of Jesus.

Be Persecuted for Living Godly

As we have already studied, persecution will come to you when you walk blessed, prosperous, victorious, and in the Word. It does not come as punishment for where you have missed it or succumbed to the flesh. Persecution comes from the ungodly for the good you have done because you have made a decision to live godly. THIS SHOULD BE ALL CHRISTIANS!

If you are going to be persecuted, then be persecuted for doing good. If doing good has nothing to do with your persecution, then such is punishment, not persecution.

Dear friends, don't be surprised at the fiery trials you are going through, as if something strange were happening to you. Instead, be very glad—for these trials make you partners with Christ in his suffering, so that you will have the wonderful joy of seeing his glory when it is revealed to all the world.

So be happy when you are insulted for being a Christian, for then the glorious Spirit of God rests upon you. If you suffer, however, it must not be for murder, stealing, making trouble, or prying into other people's affairs. But it is no shame to suffer for being a Christian. Praise God for the privilege of being called by his name! For the time has come for judgment, and it must begin with God's household. And if judgment begins with us, what terrible fate awaits those who have never obeyed God's Good News? And also, "If the righteous are barely saved, what will happen to godless sinners?"

So if you are suffering in a manner that pleases God, keep on doing what is right, and trust your lives to the God who created you, for he will never fail you.

I Peter 4:12-19, KJV

Peter is saying that if you are persecuted for doing wrong, big deal, that is nothing more than punishment, but if you are doing what is right and you are persecuted, that is different.

Wherein they think it strange that ye run not with them to the same excess of riot, speaking evil of you.

I Peter 4:4, KJV

The *New Living Translation* reads:

Of course, your former friends are surprised when you no longer plunge into the flood of wild and destructive things they do. So they slander you.

The *Contemporary English Version* interprets Peter this way:

Now your former friends wonder why you have stopped running around with them, and they curse you for it.

Peter says that your friends will not understand why you no longer party with them or do other ungodly things. Because of this, they no longer want to be your friend and will slander and persecute you. That is persecution for being godly and making a non-compromising stand.

Again, what does Jesus tell us about being persecuted?

"Rejoice and be exceedingly glad, for great is your reward in heaven, for so they persecuted the prophets who were before you."

Hallelujah! It is the ONLY way a true disciple can live.

CHAPTER 13

WALKING IN THE CHARACTER OF THE BLESSED

Walking in the character of the blessed should be an everyday demonstration for true disciples. It is the first thing Jesus teaches on the mountain, and the first thing He teaches His disciples.

Walking in the character of the blessed is walking in the ways of Jesus. It requires godly character, which begins with a godly way of thinking.

Walking in the character of the blessed requires a spiritual progression toward God first, then man. The progression aspect is key because you cannot build a relationship with man first, and then try to work in God. Such a breach in your spiritual priorities will not allow your character to develop in a way that puts God first in all things, which deprives you of a relationship with the Father, His wisdom, and His blessings.

Although we have explored this progression in the previous Chapters, let us take a moment to revisit the characteristics once again in order to gain an overall perspective of walking in the character of the blessed.

Everything in the kingdom of heaven is at your disposal.

Your progression begins with being Poor in Spirit. Poor in spirit means to be spiritually dependent on God. Jesus teaches that you will begin your spiritual progression of a true disciple when you realize in and of yourself that you can do nothing, but in Christ all things are possible.

As circumstances arise that you do not know how to handle, you will find that God ALWAYS knows what to do, and He will help you. Everything in the kingdom of heaven is at your disposal. Because you have emptied yourself out of everything except for God, and you depend solely on Him, you will have dominion in the kingdom of heaven here on earth.

"Blessed are the poor in spirit, for theirs is the kingdom of heaven."

The next step is to Mourn. After you empty yourself, the Lord begins drawing you to Him. As you begin studying the Word and discovering all God has to offer, you feel His gentle tugging. You realize where you have fallen short, and the time you wasted on the things of the world. You also view the sin of the world in its vast ugliness for the first time. Not by the standards of the world, but how those things must affect the heart of the Father. You are sorrowful because of this and for the overall condoning of sin by the Church and those around you. This all will cause you to have a godly sorrow.

Mourning, as Jesus uses the term, is not the same as the sadness you would feel when a loved one passes. We live in a day and hour when people mourn the loss of a job, economic security, and many other things. Such is not the type of mourning Jesus is talking about.

For disciples, mourning is an attitude toward sin. You can be sorrowful for sin or for the condoning of sin. Many people believe the sin of the world is not their concern because they are not involved. Jesus says that the condoning of sin should cause you to mourn as would the realization of where you, yourself, have fallen short. It is a godly sorrow that leads to repentance.

When I was born again, I was a good guy in the world's eyes. I did not smoke, drink, cuss, spit on the floor or on anyone else for that matter. I was a pretty good guy on the surface. However, when I made Jesus the Lord of my life, I had a godly sorrow for where I missed the mark for so many years.

As I began studying the Word, I wondered how things could have been different for me if I had done things God's way from day one. Where would I be now in the things of God? I am sure we would all change things and develop into the ways of God earlier if we could. Because of this you mourn. However, praise God, you do not have to stay there.

I know people who were saved 40 or 50 years ago who still have not forgiven themselves for things done before they were born again. They just beat themselves up their whole lives for past mistakes. Such is not mourning unto repentance. You have to be quick to forgive yourself and others. Then, after you repent and turn the other way, Jesus says that you will be comforted.

"Blessed are those who mourn, for they shall be comforted."

Mourning flows into Meekness. After you are comforted, you delve more into the Word of God and get busy making up for lost time. As you do so, you begin to see who you are in Christ and the blessings that are available to you. Wow! It almost seems too good to be true. You have power on earth and authority in the name of Jesus. You have ammunition against the Devil with Jesus' blood and His Word. Instead of being prideful in this power and anointing, you yield it to the Lord. Meekness is yielded strength.

When you yield your strength, all of a sudden God begins to deal with you in areas of His will concerning your growth. You could rebel at this stage and choose to resist those changes. HOWEVER, meekness says, "Yes, Lord, I hear what you are saying. I'll change that. Thank you for telling me." Meekness is nothing more than realizing that you could ignore God's instructions and continue to do things your way, but you yield.

Meekness is your attitude toward God. It is accepting His dealings no matter what. You have the power and strength to possess the earth, and you yield your power to His authority. As you do so, He will draw you even closer. Here you arrive at the throne room of God!

"Blessed are the meek, for they shall inherit the earth."

Now you Hunger and Thirst for Righteousness. It is at the throne room of God that your hunger and thirst develops for the things of God. It is a craving that cannot be filled permanently; you must eat and drink daily to be satisfied and filled. When you are at the very throne of God in His presence, you will be blessed. You will have the blessing!

As you hunger and thirst for His way of thinking and doing things, you will enjoy enviable favor and be spiritually prosperous as you deal with the issues of life. As you hunger and thirst for that kind of "rightness," He will satisfy you.

When you start to crave the Word and your relationship with the Father as you would water on a hot day, Jesus says that you will be filled.

> *Hungering and thirsting for righteousness completes your progression toward God.*

Hungering and thirsting for righteousness completes your progression toward God, and it is nothing more than putting your spiritual priorities in order. When such is the case, you shall be filled.

"Blessed are those who hunger and thirst for righteousness, for they shall be filled."

Now Mercy flows. Straight from the throne room of God, you begin your progression toward others. After being filled in the presence of the Lord, you are compassionate and merciful. You demonstrate *love in action* to those in need. In fact, you are merciful even to your enemies.

Merciful means not condemning, but understanding where others are in their walk. Further, you cannot be merciful toward someone unless you have the ability to retaliate.

God is merciful because He has the ability to retaliate against us, but He does not. True disciples sow mercy and, therefore, reap mercy.

> *"Blessed are the merciful, for they shall obtain mercy."*

Now you are Pure in Heart. As you demonstrate love in action by being merciful, your desire to help others increases. Being excited about ministering to others is a work of purity. You have a genuine godly character, which is singleness in purpose for the Lord.

Being excited about ministering to others is a work of purity.

You have cleaned your heart of all contaminates. You are not a pretender, and you do not play act. You are unmasked, unveiled, and unmixed before the Father. You are pure in heart, and you see God.

> *"Blessed are the pure in heart, for they shall see God."*

You are a Peacemaker. You no longer wish to argue or be quarrelsome. The truth of God's Word produces true peace, which is peace without compromise. You are a peacemaker. You engage in the ministry of reconciliation, with your primary focus on reconciling God with man through Jesus Christ. The world recognizes the peace on your life, and they call you a son of God.

"Blessed are the peacemakers, for they shall be called sons of God."

The Ungodly Bring Persecution. Walking in the character of the blessed brings persecution from the ungodly. But, take heart. Persecution will not stop the blessings from flowing in your life, nor the favor of God that is upon you and in you. Jesus promises this in Matthew 5:3-12, and the Bible is filled with examples of God's favor for the righteous. HOWEVER, when you follow Christ and walk out your everyday life in the character of the blessed, persecution will come for righteousness' sake and for Jesus' sake. Both come with a blessing:

"Blessed are those who are persecuted for righteousness' sake, for theirs is the kingdom of heaven.

"Blessed are you when they revile and persecute you, and say all kinds of evil against you falsely for My sake."

Persecution is the blessed result of walking in the character of the blessed. You may think "How can persecution be a blessing?" First, because Jesus says that it is a blessing, and second, because your character has developed to the point that persecution no longer bothers you. You are happy, enjoying enviable favor, and spiritual prosperity in the face of persecution. You are genuinely merciful toward those people who persecute you. That is how, through the pain of hanging crucified on a cross, Jesus is able to say,

"Father, forgive them; for they know not what they do."

Luke 23:34, KJV

Jesus is love in action! Mercy in action! Purity in action! Peacemaker in action!

What glory must have come down from that cross. Jesus' heart is FULL of mercy towards His persecutors! He has compassion! He is pure in heart! He is a peacemaker!

Jesus was willing to die on the cross to reconcile God with man and make peace. JESUS IS THE ULTIMATE PEACEMAKER!

This is how you are BLESSED when persecuted for righteousness' sake—it means you have become more like Jesus. There will be people who will say, "Well, don't you think you are high and mighty trying to be like Jesus. I remember you when you were this or that," or "Why do you want to go to church on Sunday AND Wednesday?" The more you try to adhere to the teachings of Jesus, the more this type of persecution will come. They will persecute you for righteousness' sake.

HOWEVER, once you have that settled, and your character has developed to the point where the persecution that comes for righteousness' sake no longer bothers you, then you will begin to be persecuted for Jesus' sake. *Now, pay attention because this is what I want you to catch.*

When you are persecuted for Jesus' sake, it will be because **you walk in the blessing**, and the result is envy and hate.

After you have the persecution for righteousness' sake settled (which mostly will come from other Christians, your family, and friends), then you have the world to deal with. They are going to hate you and make up lies about you. You will have to make up your mind then and there that you care more about what God thinks about you than man. And God wants you to be merciful, pure in heart, and a peacemaker toward the world.

It is human nature to want everyone to love you. I know I do. Everyone wants to be well thought of. However, if it comes to having the world's love or the Lord's love, I am going to pick His love every time. I want His fullness more than I want the love of people.

What does Jesus tell us to do in the face of persecution for His sake?

"Rejoice and be exceedingly glad, for great is your reward in heaven, for so they persecuted the prophets who were before you."

Jesus says that you will be persecuted the same as the prophets did before you. That is pretty good company. And for all who suffer persecution for Jesus' sake, GREAT is your reward in heaven.

We can only imagine what "great reward" means to Jesus. The word *great* used by Jesus in the Greek is *polus,* which means "much and many." The word *polus* is the same word used by Jesus to describe the plenteous harvest for which there are few laborers (Matt. 9:37), and the abundance of God's mercy toward us to give us His Son Jesus to bring reconciliation to man (I Pet. 1:3). Wow! That is a BIG reward.

However, Jesus does not leave us without blessings in the here and now. In addition to happiness, enjoying enviable favor, spiritual prosperity, and the power and ability to complete that which God has called us to do, Jesus promises these blessings as you develop the character of a true disciple:

- YOURS IS THE KINGDOM OF HEAVEN
- YOU ARE COMFORTED
- YOU INHERIT THE EARTH
- YOU ARE FILLED BY GOD
- YOU OBTAIN MERCY
- YOU WILL SEE GOD
- YOU ARE CALLED A SON OF GOD

What an awesome God! Imagine all of these blessings manifesting in your life at once. Such is promised to those who walk in the character of the blessed—the character of a true disciple.

CHAPTER 14

MAKE THE COMMITMENT

Jesus embodied all of the characteristics of the blessed during His earthly ministry. If it is your desire to be a disciple of Jesus Christ, you must do the same. In fact, Jesus says that His believers will do even greater works than He did because of the Holy Spirit:

> *"Most assuredly, I say to you, he who believes in Me, the works that I do he will do also; and greater works than these he will do, because I go to My Father . . . And I will pray the Father, and He will give you another Helper, that He may abide with you forever— the Spirit of truth."*
>
> John 14:12, 16-17

For a true disciple, having the characteristics of the blessed is essential.

For a true disciple, having the characteristics of the blessed is essential. They are one in the same. You cannot pick and choose which characteristics you like best and flow with them. It just does not work that way.

Once an uncompromising decision has been made to develop the character of a true disciple, there are two things you **must commit yourself to take time to do** just as Jesus did: (1) spend time alone in prayer with the Lord, and (2) spend time in the Word.

Prayer and fellowship with the Lord, as well as the earnest study of God's Word, is necessary to develop the character of the blessed. While on earth, Jesus often separated himself from the crowds to pray and spend time alone with the Father. *"Jesus was led up by the Spirit into the wilderness"* (Matt. 4:1); *"When He had come down from the mountain, great multitudes followed Him"* (Matt. 8:1); *"He went up on the mountain by Himself to pray. Now when evening came, He was alone there"* (Matt. 14:23); *"And it happened, as He was alone praying"* (Luke 9:18).

Equally important is to take the time to study your Bible and fellowship with the Father through His Word. This is fundamental. The Scriptures reveal that while on earth, Jesus had an astonishing command of the Holy Scriptures.

*And the Child grew and **became** strong in spirit, filled with wisdom; and the grace of God was upon Him . . . And when He was twelve years old, they went up to Jerusalem according to the custom of the feast . . . the Boy Jesus lingered behind in Jerusalem. And Joseph and His mother did not know it . . .*

*So when they did not find Him, they returned to Jerusalem, seeking Him. Now so it was that after three days they found Him in the temple, sitting in the midst of the teachers, both **listening to them and asking them questions.***

And all who heard Him were astonished at His understanding and answers. So when they saw Him, they were amazed; and His mother said to Him, "Son, why have You done this to us? Look, Your father and I have sought You anxiously."

And He said to them, "Why did you seek Me? Did you not know that I must be about My Father's business?"

Luke 2:40, 42-43, 45-49

I do not believe Jesus was born with the written Word already stored in His human memory. He WAS the Word made flesh (John 1:14), but from His youth, He was about His Father's business. He asked questions and listened to the teachers in the temple. He learned. He studied God's Word and the prophecies He was to fulfill.

*And He was handed the book of the prophet Isaiah. And when He had opened the book, **He found the place where it was written**: "The Spirit of the Lord is upon Me, because He has anointed Me to preach the gospel to the poor" . . . Then He closed the book, and gave it back to the attendant and sat down . . . He began to say to them, "Today this Scripture is fulfilled in your hearing."*

Luke 4:17-18, 20-21

Jesus knew where the Scripture was in the book of the prophet Isaiah. I do not believe He relied on the Spirit to know where the passage was in the Holy Scriptures. No, Jesus knew where the Scripture was because He had studied it.

It says, *"He found the place where it was written."* He had to look for the place from where He was to read.

Further, Jesus always had a ready, scriptural answer for the questions posed to Him. Jesus did not speculate or guess, and neither should we. If you do not have an answer to a question posed by someone about the Bible, tell the truth; but then, study to show yourself approved.

Study to shew thyself approved unto God, a workman that needeth not to be ashamed, rightly dividing the word of truth.

II Timothy 2:15, KJV

Paul says to be ready!

Preach the word! Be ready in season and out of season. Convince, rebuke, exhort, with all longsuffering and teaching.

II Timothy 4:2

Your primary way of learning the ways of God and fellowshipping with Him will be through the study of the Scriptures. God will speak to you primarily through His Word. If you believe God is telling you something through prayer, it must line up with His Word. This is very important to realize as your character develops and your spirit man becomes more in tune with the voice of God.

All Scripture is given by inspiration of God, and is profitable for doctrine, for reproof, for correction, for instruction in righteousness.

II Timothy 3:16, KJV

> *Being submitted to your pastor will help keep you out of a spiritual ditch.*

Jesus has given us all pastors to assist with our development as true disciples here on earth. Being submitted to your pastor will help keep you out of a spiritual ditch.

If something you believe you heard from the Lord does not line up with the Word, or if you are not sure, seek the counsel of your pastor. He is there to guide you. If you do not have a pastor, by the Spirit of God go find one! Television preachers cannot pastor you, although they can provide you with wonderful teaching.

He who descended is also the One who ascended far above all the heavens, that He might fill all things.

*And **He Himself** gave some to be apostles, some prophets, some evangelists, and some pastors and teachers, **for the equipping of the saints for the work of ministry**.*

Ephesians 4:10-12

Prayer of Commitment

Whether you are a new Christian or have been serving the Lord for years, if you would like to begin walking in the character of the blessed, the time to start is now. There will never be easy or perfect conditions to adhere to the teachings of Jesus or dedicate your life to Him.

True disciples are not always called to the mission fields or into full-time ministry. Jesus needs true disciples walking among the lost everywhere. True disciples are the salt of the earth (Matt. 5:13). Pray this prayer with me:

Father, in the name of Jesus Christ of Nazareth, I thank You for bringing this revelation to me today concerning walking in the character of the blessed. I thank You for those blessings and the opportunity to serve You in a more committed way.

I make a commitment to watch my thought life and to fill my heart with Your Word because it is from my heart that my character and issues of life flow. I want them to be uncompromising to the Word of God. No fear!

As I yield myself to You, by faith I pour out myself to You. I know that I can do nothing without You and that I am spiritually dependent on You for all things.

Thank You for Your guidance in this transformation of my life. I thank You that I am no longer

deceived in any way concerning self-importance. It is my desire to be poor in spirit. I desire to mourn unto godly sorrow for where I have missed it and for the sin of the world. I desire to yield myself to You in meekness. I desire to hunger and thirst for righteousness and meet You in Your throne room!

Then, I ask that You fill me, so I can be merciful to others, pure in heart with singleness in purpose for You, and reconcile those to You as a peacemaker. I forgive those in advance whom Satan and his demon cohorts use to persecute me for either righteousness' sake or Jesus' sake. It does matter which. I purpose myself not to be moved off course by persecution. I yield myself to You, Father, in Jesus' mighty name.

I hereby clear my conscience and repent for any wrong doing. Whether it was an intentional act or one through ignorance, I cover those deeds with the shed blood of Jesus. I ask for Your forgiveness and accept Your forgiveness because You are merciful and just to forgive those who ask, and that is me today.

Use me to further the good news of reconciliation of You to man through our Lord and Savior, Jesus Christ. Thank you for the opportunity to have the blessed character of a true disciple. It is my wish to be about Your business. I look to You and welcome guidance every step of the way.

Thank You, Heavenly Father. In Jesus' name, Amen.

Now, with God the Father, God the Son, and God the Holy Spirit as your witness, it is my prayer that you find yourself calm, full of peace, and of good conscience. May the light of your love walk outshine any envy, malice, or anger that others have because you are walking blessed as a true disciple.

I set my prayer with yours. Go forth and prosper. Read this book again, along with your Bible, so the instructions can become part of your daily walk as you spiritually progress into the *Character of the Blessed.*

ABOUT THE AUTHOR

D r. **Billy J. Rash** is Senior Pastor of Kern Christian Center in Bakersfield, California. He earned a Doctorate of Divinity from Southern California Theological Seminary and a Doctorate of Theology from Vision Christian University.

After accepting the Lord and receiving the baptism of the Holy Spirit in the early 1970s, Pastor Billy Rash was introduced to the faith message through the ministry of Kenneth Copeland. Pastor Billy went to work for Kenneth Copeland Ministries as an Associate Minister in 1978. If Gloria Copeland could not attend a meeting, then Pastor Billy would teach the healing school and participate in the miracle services with Brother Copeland.

In the following years, he began evangelizing under Billy Rash Ministries. In 1985, Pastor Billy moved to Bakersfield and started a new church, Kern Christian Center.

In addition to his duties as Senior Pastor, he is also involved in community service as Chaplain for the Bakersfield Police Department. He is on the President's Cabinet for Jerry Savelle Ministries. Pastor Billy is married to Shelby Rash, and they make their home in Bakersfield, California.

Audio and video messages from Pastor Billy can be accessed via the Internet at www.kernchristiancenter.org.

For more information, please contact:
Billy Rash Ministries
7850 White Lane, No. 117
Bakersfield, California 93309

(661) 664-1000

BOOKS BY DR. BILLY RASH:

THE CHARACTER OF THE BLESSED
(The Power of the Reborn Spirit)

———————

THE WAY OF CAIN
(Breaking the Cycle of Self-Deception)

Now Available!

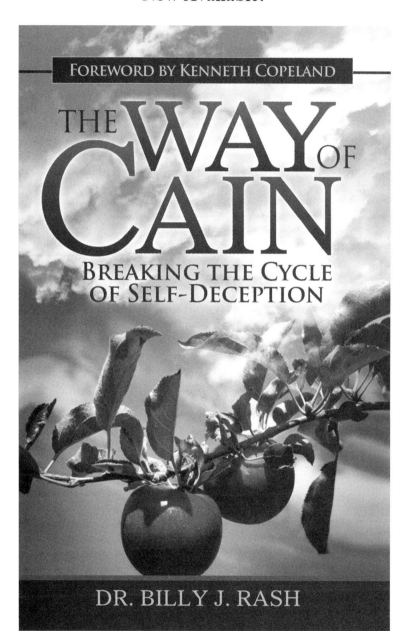